THE EMPEROR WHO ATE THE BIBLE

D O U B L E D A Y

NEW YORK

LONDON

TORONTO

SYDNEY

AUCKLAND

✦✦✦✦✦✦✦✦✦✦✦✦✦✦✦✦✦✦✦✦✦✦✦✦✦✦✦✦

THE
EMPEROR
WHO
ATE
THE BIBLE

AND MORE STRANGE FACTS AND
USELESS INFORMATION

SCOT MORRIS

PUBLISHED BY DOUBLEDAY
a division of Bantam Doubleday Dell Publishing Group, Inc.
666 Fifth Avenue, New York, New York 10103

DOUBLEDAY and the portrayal of an anchor
with a dolphin are trademarks of Doubleday,
a division of Bantam Doubleday Dell
Publishing Group, Inc.

Library of Congress Cataloging-in-Publication Data
Morris, Scot.
The emperor who ate the Bible, and more
strange facts and useless information / Scot
Morris. —1st ed.
p.   cm.
1. Curiosities and wonders.   I. Title.
AG243.M675   1991
031.02—dc20   90-31233
                                      CIP

ISBN 0-385-26755-X

BOOK DESIGN BY CAROL A. MALCOLM

1   3   5   7   9   10   8   6   4   2
First Edition

Dedicated to
Martin Gardner, Friend and Inspiration

Thanks to
Sabra Moore and James Cravens

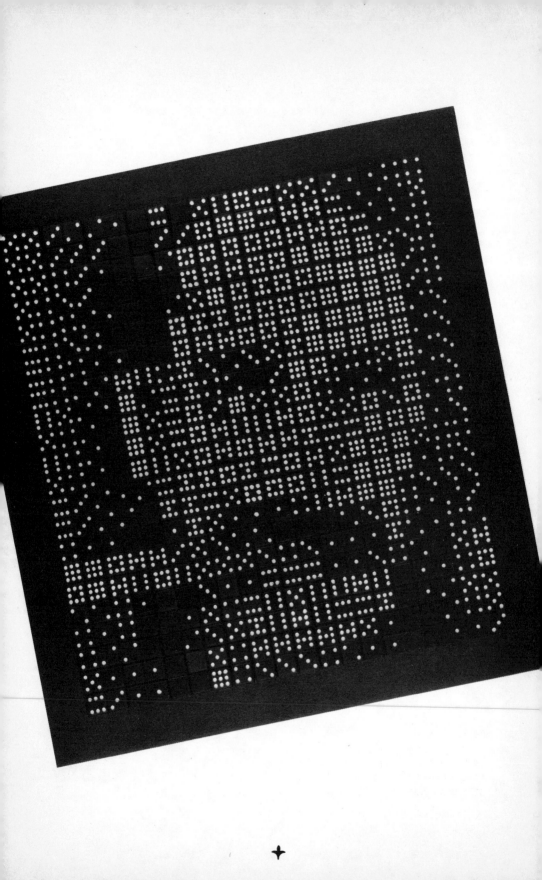

WHO'S THAT IN THE DOMINOES?

Ken Knowlton created the image here (facing page) entirely out of dominoes. Look closely and you'll see 220 dominoes, some vertical and some horizontal, carefully arranged inside a rectangle 22 inches tall and 20 inches wide. Step back and you see a face. Farther still and you recognize the face: Groucho Marx.

Knowlton first took the Groucho image, marked it off into a grid of squares and assigned each square a "shade of gray" value, on a ten-point scale from black to white. He could have made it easy on himself and picked dominoes for their desired shades— blank-blank ones for the all-black areas, double-fives and double-sixes for the mid-gray areas, and double-nines for the whitest areas of the picture, for example.

But Knowlton wanted more of a challenge. He designed the portrait to be made out of precisely 220 dominoes—four complete sets of double-nine dominoes with 55 pieces in each set, in all combinations from blank-blank up to nine-nine. The computer program had to find the best place for each of the tiles, including the difficult ones like the blank-nine, the one-eight, and so on. It also had to find the optimal orientation of each tile—either horizontal or vertical—and whenever one tile was changed, the other tiles had to be reshuffled to keep everything within the borders. ~Photo courtesy of Ken Knowlton

Rhode Island prison inmates have the legal right to change their underwear once a week.

When Major Clark Gable left the Army in June 1944 his discharge papers were signed by Captain Ronald Reagan.

A PROPHETESS WITH BAD VISION

}I n 1857, a fourteen-year-old girl named Nongqawuse, of the Gealeke Xhosa tribe in South Africa, had a revelation. She said she saw the faces of the tribe's dead elders staring back at her from the surface of the river Gxara. The deceased could come back, she told her fellow Xhosans, if the tribe slaughtered all of their livestock by February 18. The Xhosans believed in the girl's vision, and did as directed.

After the big slaughter, when the departed leaders didn't come back, the tribesmen realized that the sacrifice hadn't worked and that the young girl's vision had been mistaken, to put it mildly. As a result of following her directions, the entire tribe starved to death.

}T hat death-defying, lady-killing master spy 007 was the fictional namesake of a bird fancier. One of Ian Fleming's favorite books was *Birds of the West Indies*, written by a naturalist named James Bond.

}A glacier in the Beartooth Mountains of Montana is filled with two-hundred-year-old grasshoppers. An enormous swarm of the insects apparently landed on the surface of the ice two centuries ago, and were quick-frozen by a sudden snowstorm. The grasshoppers are so well preserved that as the glacier melts, birds and bears come to feed on them.

}A mosquito has forty-seven teeth.

Quiz. *There's one sport in which neither the spectators nor the participants know the score or the leader until the contest ends. What is it? (Answer: page 15)*

"I FEEL PRETTY AND I COULD HAVE DANCED ALL NIGHT"

}T hat wasn't Natalie Wood you heard singing in *West Side Story*, and it wasn't Audrey Hepburn singing in *My Fair Lady*, either. The dubbed voice of soprano Marni Nixon was on the soundtrack of both films.

ODD QUESTION, DIPLOMATIC ANSWER

Henry Kissinger once asked Chou En-lai to speculate on what might have happened if Nikita Khrushchev had been assassinated instead of JFK. Chou thought a moment, then said, "I don't believe Mr. Onassis would have married Mrs. Khrushchev."

66 *Come, come! Why, they couldn't hit an elephant at this dist—* **99**
~the last words of General John Sedgwick, attempting to rally his troops, Spotsylvania, May 9, 1864

The one millionth trademark registered by the U.S. Patent Office was for Sweet 'N Low.

The most heavily used pay phone in the United States, according to AT&T figures, is the one near the ticket office at the Greyhound Bus station in downtown Chicago. An average of 270 calls are made on it a day.

Claude Monet was painting an enormous tree near Giverny, France, in the spring of 1883 when

In 1950, Ralph Edwards, host of the hit radio show "Truth or Consequences," offered free publicity to any town that would change its name to the name of his program. Hot Springs, New Mexico, quickly volunteered, and the town has been Truth or Consequences, New Mexico, ever since. It's still there on Interstate 25, between Albuquerque and Las Cruces. The townsfolk were proud of their decision. The park in the center of town is Ralph Edwards Park.
~Photo courtesy of The Herald, Truth or Consequences, N.M.

three weeks of rain set in and stopped his work. When Monet was able to return to his easel the tree had fully bloomed. At the artist's request the mayor of Giverny organized a work party that removed every leaf and bud from the tree so Monet could finish his painting.

.{Abraham Lincoln moved his lips when he read.

❝We used to have a dog named Snoopy, you know, a real live dog. I suppose people who love Snoopy won't like it, but we gave him away. He fought with other dogs, so we traded him in for a load of gravel. ❞
~Charles Schulz

Gardenias and orange blossoms both have lovely fragrances, but combine the two flowers in a bouquet and the smells neutralize each other. The bouquet will have no aroma at all.

Bing Crosby thought his ears stuck out too far. He glued them down with spirit gum for his early movie appearances. Later in his career, the confident crooner let his ears stick out for all to see. ~Photo courtesy of Culver Pictures

HOT DOG HISTORY

"Red hots! Get your red-hot dachshund sausages here!" Vendors at the New York Polo Grounds, around the turn of the century, used that call on cold days to attract customers for their frankfurters. The German sausages were called dachshunds, quite naturally, after the German dog with the similar elongated shape.

Sports humorist T. A. "Tad" Dorgan was amused by the scene and drew a cartoon of it: a barking dachshund in a bread roll. Dorgan didn't know how to spell "dachshund," so he called the creature a "hot dog" in the caption. The new name caught on and endured.

The largest iceberg ever seen was spotted floating in the South Pacific in 1956. It was 208 miles long and 60 miles wide, larger than Belgium.

Rin Tin Tin died in 1932 in Jean Harlow's arms.

In 1919 a hydrofoil boat set a world's water speed record of over seventy miles per hour. The boat's creator and pilot, seventy-two years old and already world-famous at the time, was Alexander Graham Bell.

In *Mein Kampf* Adolf Hitler incorporated some anti-Semitic opinions he had gotten from an admired source—Henry Ford. Hitler kept a framed photo of Ford on his desk in Berlin, and Ford, who made substantial contributions to the Nazi party, kept a portrait of Hitler on his desk in Dearborn, Michigan.

ICE ADVICE

The U.S. Navy's *Polar Manual*, the official handbook for sailors assigned to duty in the Arctic or Antarctic, offers this sensible warning: "Do not touch cold metal with moist, bare hands. If you should inadvertently stick a hand to cold metal, urinate on the metal to warm it and save some inches of skin. If you stick both hands, you'd better have a friend along."

Quiz. What famous North American landmark is constantly moving backward? (Answer: page 15)

CHE'S WORST ASTHMA ATTACK

{ A }sthma isn't often fatal, but it was to Ernesto "Che" Guevara, the revolutionary leader and key figure in Fidel Castro's Cuba. When Guevara was hiding in Bolivia in 1967, he carried a small wood stove with him and set it up at camps to help him relieve his breathing difficulties in the humid jungle. He was located by an infrared camera on a U-2 spy plane that registered the stove's heat. He was then trapped and killed by a Special Forces Unit of the U.S. Army.

•{ L }ee Trevino's tongue-in-cheek advice to anyone caught on a golf course during a thunder-and-lightning storm: "Stand in the middle of the fairway and hold up a one-iron. Not even God can hit a one-iron."

{ R }oses cut in the afternoon last longer than roses cut in the morning.

{ A }ccording to American funeral directors, corpses aren't decomposing as rapidly as they used to. The undertakers think it has something to do with more food preservatives in the American diet.

•{ T }he first precise calculation of the height of Mount Everest came out to 29,000 feet exactly. The surveyors are said to have falsified the total and published it as 29,020 feet, because that figure looked more exact and less like a "rounded off" estimate.

NOT RIGHT FOR THE PART

{ W }hen United Artists was casting the 1964 film *The Best Man*, about a white U.S. President with a black VP, someone suggested Ronald Reagan be offered the starring role. The UA executive dismissed the idea, explaining, "Reagan doesn't have the presidential look."

{ A }ccording to *TV Guide*, an Irish medical researcher studied women who regularly watched favorite soap operas during their pregnancies. Their babies later seemed to recognize the theme music to those shows: they would calm down and stop crying the moment the shows began. The baby doctor called this effect "fetal 'soap' addiction."

. { Greensleeves," the ancient English folk song (it was one of Shakespeare's favorites), and the Christmas carol "What Child Is This?" have two entirely different sets of lyrics and the same melody.

FLIGHT STIMULATOR

{ Blow on a locust and it will flap its wings. This migratory grasshopper has a bundle of hairs on its head that responds to a head-on air current by sending a nerve impulse to the wings, making them beat. This reflex leads to flying, of course, which increases the head-on breeze, which stimulates the locust to keep flapping. The feedback mechanism keeps these insects flying for great distances.

The black rhinoceros may look like a brute and weigh more than a ton, but surprisingly, it is one of the most docile animals in Africa. In captivity the animal becomes so gentle it is happy to eat out of its keeper's hand, and it loves to have its ears rubbed. ~Photo by R. Van Gelder, courtesy of Department Library Sciences, American Museum of Natural History

RARE BIT OF ETYMOLOGY

Any restaurant that lists "Welsh rarebit" on its menu doesn't get the joke. The original name for this dish was "Welsh rabbit," an English putdown of the Welsh implying that citizens of Wales could afford nothing finer to eat than melted cheese. "Rarebit" has no meaning in English except as a euphemism, a way of making cookbooks and menus less offensive and patronizing.

As a cultural comment, "Welsh rabbit" is in the same category as "Bombay duck," which contains no duck, and "Salisbury steak," which is just ground beef. A similar sarcastic spirit inspired the name for a buzzing "raspberry" noise made with the lips and tongue and intended to be insulting: the "Bronx cheer."

A WOMAN NOT TO BE BELIEVED

After she was appointed Shadow Spokesman on Education, Margaret Thatcher was interviewed in the London Sunday Telegraph, *October 26, 1969. On the subject of women in British politics, Thatcher had these observations: "No woman in my time will be Prime Minister or Chancellor or Foreign Secretary—not the top jobs. Anyway, I wouldn't want to be Prime Minister: you have to give yourself 100 percent."* ~Photo courtesy of UPI/Bettmann Newsphotos

The animal with the largest penis in relation to its body size is the flea.

When Felix Mendelssohn wrote an orchestral piece to celebrate the art of painting he knew that the melody was so good that someone would eventually want to sing it. He had some definite opinions about what he wanted in the way of future lyrics: "There must be a national and merry subject found out, something to which the soldierlike and buxom motion of the piece has some relation, and the words must express something gay and popular, as the music tries to do."

Charles Wesley honored the composer's request when he turned Mendelssohn's tune into a Christmas carol with these opening lines: "Hark! the herald angels sing, Glory to the newborn king!"

Lighting a cigar with a hundred-dollar bill, that grand gesture of the tycoon, can be performed legally and at no cost if you blow out your light in time. So long as you save more than half of any damaged bill in recognizable form, you can exchange it for a new one at any Federal Reserve bank.

General Douglas MacArthur was dressed in skirts by his mother until he was eight.

Tennis ace Evonne Goolagong's last name means "kangaroo's nose" in Australia's aboriginal language.

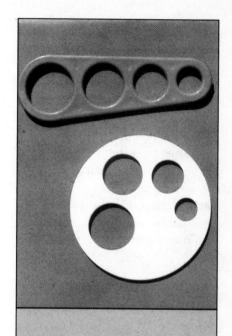

Whatzit Quiz

These four-holed plastic objects aren't modern art pieces, they're kitchen tools. The white disc is about five inches in diameter. What are the implements used for? (Answer: page 15) ~Photo by Scot Morris

The Alexander Column in Leningrad was built in 1834 during a bitterly cold winter. Workers mixed mortar for the bricks with vodka instead of water to keep it from freezing.

·}A printer's error changed the name of a future Nobel prizewinner. William Faulkner was born William Falkner, descended from generations of Falkners who all spelled the name without a u. When the novelist's first book was published a printer's typo misspelled the author's surname *Faulkner*. William thought it over, decided he liked the look of his new name, and became William Faulkner thereafter.

}Polk County, Florida, grows more oranges per year than does the entire state of California.

&&Don't let it end like this. Tell them I said something.**
~last words of Pancho Villa (1878–1923)

Quiz· Of all vegetables, only two can live to produce on their own for several growing seasons. All other vegetables must be replanted every year. What are the only two perennial vegetables? (Answer: page 15)

}Gustave Eiffel—of Eiffel Tower fame—was a contributing designer for the Statue of Liberty. He designed the steel bracing that holds together Miss Liberty's upraised right arm.

·}The notebooks in which Marie and Pierre Curie recorded their historic experiments on radium, three quarters of a century ago, are still radioactive.

}Because the disease was thought to be influenced by the stars, it was named influenza in the Middle Ages.

}The man failed in business at age 22, was defeated for the legislature at 23, and failed again in business at 24. He was elected to the legislature at 25, but suffered a nervous breakdown at 27, and was defeated for Speaker at 29, Elector at 31, and Congress at 34. After winning a term in Congress at 37, he lost the seat at 39, lost a Senate race at 46, was passed over for Vice President at 47, and lost another race for the Senate at 49. It doesn't seem like a very distinguished résumé, but it belongs to Abraham Lincoln.

THE WONDER YEARS

·{ What's the safest time in a person's life? Actuarial tables show that a person in this country has the greatest chance of staying alive another year at nine, ten, and eleven than at any other age. These are the years with the lowest mortality rates. After eleven, it's all downhill.

{ The party that enlivens New Orleans every spring has two names—Carnival and Mardi Gras —both of which refer to dietary rules for the period that preceded Lent in the medieval church calendar. The word *carnival* comes from the Latin and means "removal of meat." In New Orleans the festival lasts about ten days, with the final day being "Fat Tuesday," the last day to gorge oneself on meat before the forty-day fast preceding Easter. In French, "fat Tuesday" is *mardi gras*. Over the years, the name for the last day of the festivities has come to be used for the entire party period.

{ During World War II it was discovered that the liquid inside young coconuts can be used as a substitute for blood plasma in an emergency.

·{ It is illegal to fall asleep under a hair dryer in Florida.

{ Each edition of Who's Who in America contains several biographies of fictitious persons with the address of a real Who's Who employee. This is done to discourage those who would use the publication to compile mailing lists of the rich and famous. If the employee finds himself on a mailing list under the false name, the Who's Who lawyers go into action.

{ One *nebuchadnezzar*, the largest champagne container, holds 104 glasses of bubbly. Next comes the 83-glass *balthazar*, the 62-glass *salmanazar*, the 41-glass *methuselah*, the 31-glass *rehoboam*, the 21-glass *jeroboam*, and the 10-glass *magnum*. The puny little *bottle* of champagne holds a mere 5 glasses.

Quiz. Name the country in which each of the following dishes originated:
Swiss steak
Russian dressing
chop suey
vichyssoise
(Answers: page 15)

{Muhammad Ali's great-great-grandfather was a slave owned by an early abolitionist, Cassius Marcellus Clay, who was ambassador to Russia in the 1860s. One of Ali's great-grandfathers was a white Irishman named Grady.

{Pollen is forever. It's one of the few natural substances that will not deteriorate.

PERSISTENT PEST

{Householders battling cockroaches may have suspected the insects are indestructible—and they almost are. There are thirty-five hundred species of cockroach, thriving in every region on this planet except at the Poles. Cockroaches can survive by eating paper, glue, or soap if no other food is available. They can live for as long as five months without food, one month without water. They can tolerate several times the radiation that would kill a human being, and one species can revive itself, apparently with no ill effects, after being frozen for forty-eight hours.

A beheaded cockroach, in fact, can survive and continue to perform most bodily functions—including reproduction—until it finally dies of starvation. Researchers at Michigan State University found that headless cockroaches could be conditioned to avoid electric shock faster than roaches that still had their heads intact.

{By coincidence, several terms that are common to music are also used in the game of baseball. Here are five, for example: run, pitch, slide, score, tie, and base (bass).

{Among the hate mail received by Harriet Beecher Stowe after the publication of *Uncle Tom's Cabin* was one package containing the ear of a slave.

{Lewis Carroll is said to have taken many of the characters in *Alice in Wonderland* from apparitions that came to him before attacks of migraine headaches.

Quiz Answers

Page 4: Boxing.

Page 7: Niagara Falls. The rim is being worn down by the millions of gallons of water that rush over it every minute, and the falls recede about two and a half feet a year. At that rate, the falls will meet up with Lake Erie (now about twenty miles away) in forty thousand years or so.

Page 11: They're spaghetti measurers. Whether thin or thick pasta is being used, the amount of stiff dry sticks that will fit through the smallest hole is a two-ounce portion. The holes grow in size at two-ounce intervals, so the largest hole measures an eight-ounce serving of pasta.

Page 12: Asparagus and rhubarb.

Page 13: All four dishes were invented in the United States.

That *zombie vampire in the 1939 film*
Return of Dr. X *is the young Hum-*
phrey Bogart. ~Photo courtesy of Culver Pictures

CHAPTER 2

When Top 40 deejay Casey Kasem wed Jean Thompson in 1980, the ceremony was performed by Jesse Jackson.

In one survey of first-graders, a large percentage chose *Diarrhea* as the most poetic-sounding female name.

THE ETHIOPIAN EMPEROR'S CURE

The African ruler who beat the Italian army at Adwa in 1896 and established the country of Ethiopia was Emperor Menelik II. He believed that the Bible had curative powers and he would eat a few pages of it to help restore his health whenever he felt sick. After a stroke in 1913 he ate the entire Book of Kings, suffered the complications of a bowel obstruction, and died.

When George Bernard Shaw was offered England's prestigious Order of Merit, he turned it down. "It would be superfluous, as I have already conferred this order on myself," he explained.

❝ What a glorious garden of wonders this would be to anyone who was lucky enough not to be able to read. ❞
~G. K. Chesterton, on seeing the lights of Broadway's Great White Way, 1921

BLINKING BUGS

You can tell a glowworm's sex by the frequency of its light flashes. Male glowworms flash every 5.8 seconds, females every 2.1 seconds.

Of all the water on this planet—in oceans, lakes, rivers, clouds, and so on—only 3 percent is fresh water.

ALL CLEAR NOW?

"Tenses, gender, and number: For the purpose of the rules and regulations contained in this chapter, the present tense includes the past and future tenses, and the future the present; the masculine gender includes the feminine and the feminine the masculine; and the singular includes the plural and the plural the singular."
~a "clarification" of terms in the California State Code of the Division of Consumer Services, Department of Consumer Affairs

Tidal waves on the open ocean sometimes reach speeds of more than five hundred nautical miles per hour.

The Bridge of Eggs can be found in Lima, Peru. In 1610 it was built of mortar mixed not with water but with the whites of ten thousand eggs.

DISARMING ANALOGY

Elbridge Gerry, a Founding Father, governor of Massachusetts, and eventually Vice President of the United States under James Madison, believed strongly that the country should avoid a military buildup. At the Constitutional Convention of 1787 he argued that the U.S. Army should be limited to no more than three hundred men in peacetime. He made his case vociferously by comparing military might with a male erection: "A standing army is like a standing member," he said. "It's an excellent assurance of domestic tranquility, but a dangerous temptation to foreign adventure."

Most American automobile horns honk in the key of F.

Hummingbirds can't walk.

"CAST IT AGAIN, SAM"

Hollywood directors wanted Ronald Reagan, not Humphrey Bogart, to be the star of *Casablanca*. First choices were also Gregory Peck for *The African Queen* and George Raft for *The Maltese Falcon*. Bogie, the immortal cinema icon, was almost never the first choice of casting directors of his day.

HEALTHY JAWS

The great white shark is not only nature's supreme killing machine, it is also one of her most indestructible specimens. The great white is one of the few animals known to be completely immune to cancer; and special antibodies give this species immunity to almost every known bacterial disease as well.

Quiz· As the sun goes behind a cloud or a mountain range, rays of sunlight flare out across the sky as in this photo, an effect called the "Rays of Buddha." But the sun is 93 million miles away, and its rays are parallel by the time they reach Earth. So why do the rays "diverge," or spread out, when they hit a cloud, as seen here? (Answer: page 29) ~Photo by Scot Morris

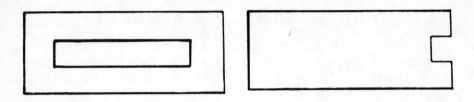

FRONT   SIDE

Quiz. Here are two views of the same object. Can you tell what the whole object looks like? Draw a picture of it as seen from another angle. (Answer: page 29)

CHANGE OF MENU

At Delmonico's restaurant in New York, shipping magnate Charles Wenburg showed the owner a new way of preparing lobster that he had discovered on his travels in South America. Lorenzo Delmonico loved the recipe and added it to his menu under the name "lobster Wenburg." Weeks later Wenburg got into a brawl in the restaurant and had to be thrown out. As punishment, Delmonico changed his menu the next day, reversing the first three letters of Wenburg's name. The dish became "lobster Newburg" and has been known by that name ever since.

Geology students at the University of California, Santa Cruz, discovered three earthquake faults on campus. The first was named "McHenry's Fault" in honor of the chancellor. The other two were named "My Fault" and "Your Fault."

A BABY CAN, BUT YOU CAN'T

If you try to breathe and swallow at the same time, you will find that you cannot. You did have this ability, however, up until the age of six or seven months, possibly to make nursing easier.

{ No matter what the romantic songs say, no bride has ever walked down the aisle. Aisles are walkways down both sides of a church next to the walls. Brides walk down the nave.

Quiz. True or false: Alfred Lord Tennyson wrote "The Charge of the Heavy Brigade." (Answer: page 29)

{ San Francisco's favorite song wasn't exactly an instant smash. George Cory wrote the words to "I Left My Heart in San Francisco" (the tune was by Douglass Cross) when he was suffering homesickness while in New York in 1946. It remained unrecorded for fifteen long years. Then Tony Bennett introduced it in his act at San Francisco's Fairmont Hotel in 1961. It became an "overnight" hit, and San Francisco adopted it as the city's official song eight years later.

"I Left My Heart in San Francisco" was the only hit song George Cory ever wrote. He died of a medication overdose in 1978—in San Francisco.

"I DIDN'T *KILL HIM.* YEAH . . . THAT'S IT, THAT'S THE TICKET."

{ In 1821, a man named Desjardins was arrested for the murder of the Duc de Berry, and he confessed to the crime. Later, he retracted his confession on most unusual grounds—that he was a pathological liar. In his defense at the court trial, witness after witness swore that Desjardins was unreliable, a known liar, and shouldn't be believed. The jury believed Desjardins' defense and found him not guilty.

NO YOLK

{ Eggs can be frozen whole for up to nine months with no detriment to their quality. When freezing raw eggs, be sure to put them in a container that will allow half an inch of space or more around each egg as it expands.

{ Joan of Arc was historically insignificant until the nineteenth century when Napoleon needed a hero-figure to arouse French nationalism and resurrected her legend. At the time of her martyrdom Joan was not even French. She was born in 1412 in Domrémy, an independent state then totally outside French jurisdiction.

King Ranch in Texas, at 1.25 million acres, is bigger than the state of Rhode Island. It was the first completely fenced-in ranch in the world.

HOW ABOUT "COLD ENOUGH FOR YOU?"

Alaska is the only state without an official motto.

Dancing to "The Star-Spangled Banner" is against the law in several states.

Quiz. In what country are Japanese people Caucasians? (Answer: page 29)

FEET FEAT

The *entrechat dix* is a ballet move in which the dancer crosses and uncrosses his or her legs ten times during a single leap. Only one person in history has been able to do it—the Russian Vaslav Nijinsky, who died in 1950.

THE MEASURE OF A MAN

Henry Cavendish, in his pioneering studies of electricity in the eighteenth century, at first had no physical measurement of the strength of an electrical current, so he used his own body. He shocked himself with different amounts of current and estimated the pain. Cavendish lived to the ripe age of seventy-nine.

The suggestion may have been half in jest, but we suspect educators around the world would approve. J. V. Walker, a public health officer in England, wanted scientists to develop a pill that would delay puberty in students until after they had graduated from college.

A rat can go without water longer than a camel can.

How long can a fire burn? A fire in a coal mine near Straitsville, Ohio, burned for fifty-two years. Measures were finally taken to put it out after it began to threaten hundreds of homes in the area.

The only mammal with a poisonous bite is the short-tailed shrew. ~Photo by Herbert Lang, courtesy of the Department of Library Services, American Museum of Natural History

PLASTIC PRIZE

Celluloid, the first synthetic plastic, was invented by John Wesley Hyatt in the early 1860s. He won a $10,000 prize for it, in a contest to develop a substitute for ivory billiard balls.

William Shakespeare may have been one of the greatest writers in history, but he failed as a writer of history. In Julius Caesar, Shakespeare refers to a clock that strikes the hour—but striking clocks weren't invented for another fourteen hundred years after Caesar. He mentions the game of billiards in Antony and Cleopatra, a cannon in King John, and turkeys in 1 Henry IV, but none of those things had been invented or discovered at the time each play was supposed to take place.

Shakespeare's geography was off, too. In Coriolanus he calls Delphi an island; it's a city. In The Winter's Tale he writes of a vessel "driven by storm on the coast of Bohemia," and has Antigonus say, "Our ship hath touch'd upon the deserts of Bohemia." The trouble is, Bohemia (now part of Czechoslovakia) is a landlocked area—it doesn't have a coast, so no ship could ever come close to its deserts.

Finally, the Bard's writing was itself surprisingly inconsistent. Shakespeare spelled his own name four different ways in his handwritten will.

PASS THE ZEAXANTHIN, PLEASE

·} People who buy only "natural" foods with "no chemicals" often forget that everything we eat is made of chemicals. Would you eat a meal that contained methanol, acetaldehyde, ovomucoid, zeaxanthin, succinic acid, anisyl propionate, and malic acid? This ingredient list would scare off any conscientious shopper, but according to Panic in the Pantry: Food Facts, Fads, and Fallacies, these are just some of the chemicals in a simple breakfast of coffee, eggs, and melon.

} It is illegal to attend the theater within four hours of eating garlic in Gary, Indiana.

The famous painting Washington Crossing the Delaware by Emanuel Leutze depicts a dramatic moment in the American Revolution, but the artist took several liberties with history. The crossing was in 1776, but the Stars and Stripes flag shown wasn't adopted until the next year. The real boats were forty to sixty feet long, larger than the rather insubstantial ones shown; the soldiers wouldn't have held their rifles pointing upward, so that snow and sleet could get in the barrels; and Washington certainly knew not to stand, a pose that would make the boat unstable and put himself in danger of falling overboard. Leutze did the painting in Düsseldorf, and used the Rhine, not the Delaware, as his model river.
~Photo courtesy of The Metropolitan Museum of Art, gift of John S. Kennedy, 1897

A classic Christmas carol was tossed off in three hours on December 24, 1818. Austrian priest Joseph Mohr learned on Christmas Eve that his church organ wasn't working. He wanted music for his scheduled services that night, so he went to his friend Franz Gruber's house, and the two men quickly composed a song. At midnight mass they sang it with guitar accompaniment—the first public performance of "Silent Night."

Franklin D. Roosevelt, perhaps the most popular U.S. President, won an unprecedented four terms in office. The folks back home weren't all that impressed, however. In not one of those elections did he carry his home county of Dutchess in New York.

On June 12, 1775, the British offered to pardon any colonist who surrendered. Only two men were not to receive this amnesty: Samuel Adams and John Hancock. If captured they were to be hanged.

The future comedian was born Cornelius Crane Chase. He got the nickname "Chevy" from his grandmother.

Quiz. *Which state capital is located on the Colorado River? (Answer: page 29)*

Hoyt Wilhelm was one of the best relief pitchers in baseball history. He pitched in 1,070 games, a career-high record. In his first time at bat, in 1952, he hit a home run. He never hit another one in his entire twenty-one-year career. His lifetime batting average was only .088.

A wristwatch that monitors the wearer's pulse, and sounds an alarm when the heartbeat becomes abnormal, was invented by Herbert Marx. He was better known as Zeppo, the fourth Marx Brother.

During the Revolutionary War, the governor of New Jersey was a Tory arrested for treasonous support of the British. He wasn't executed because of the importance of his father. Instead, he was exchanged for American prisoners and later escaped to England. The traitor was Benjamin Franklin's son William.

{ Don't forget the following important legal holidays from various states:

Fast Day
(fourth Monday in April—New Hampshire)

Repudiation Day
(November 23—Maryland)

Cherokee Strip Day
(September 16—Oklahoma)

Kamehameha Day
(June 11—Hawaii)

Nathan B. Forrest's Birthday
(July 13—Tennessee)

Will Rogers Day
(November 4—Oklahoma)

{ In the seventeenth century, Englanders who considered the exiled Catholic Stuarts to be the real claimants to the English throne drank their royal toasts in a special, secret way. They would hold their glasses above their water bowls to show that the toast was really for the king "over the water," as in "across the sea." The secret got out and such a toast was considered an act of treason then; so tables were set without water bowls. It is still considered a breach of etiquette to have finger bowls on the table when a British king or queen is present.

{ The first full-length movie shown on American TV was not one of Hollywood's finest. A fitting precursor to today's sleep-inducing "Late, Late Show" and "Midnight Movie," it was titled The Heart of New York, the story of the invention of the washing machine.

{ When Albert Einstein was on his deathbed, he said something in German. The nurse who was attending him didn't speak German, so no one will ever know what the great scientist's last words were.

DO YOU HAVE A GRAY THUMB? TRY PLANTING THESE.

{ Inept home gardeners are advised to invest in the aptly named cast-iron plant (aspidistra). A cast-iron plant can tolerate months of neglect, low light, insufficient water, and low humidity, which makes it the ideal vegetable companion for the modern homemaker on the go. The only houseplant that might be considered more durable is sold by some florists as an "air fern." It can't be killed because it is already dead.

By coincidence, Disneyland and Walt Disney World are in counties with the same name. The former is in Orange County, California, the latter in Orange County, Florida.

GUARDIANS OF DECENCY

The National Association of Broadcasters forbids showing gargling on television.

When Benjamin Disraeli received unsolicited books for his review, he would send this ingeniously worded acknowledgment: "Thank you very much for sending me the book. I shall lose no time in reading it."

THE RECORD RECORD

In this century, only one athlete has set more than one world's record in track and field in a single day. On May 25, 1935, at the Big Ten conference championships at Ann Arbor, Michigan, Jesse Owens broke records in the 100-yard dash, the broad jump, the 220-yard dash, and the 220-yard hurdles. He set four new world's records in just forty-five minutes.

Parker Brothers prints more money each year for its Monopoly games than the U.S. Government issues in real currency.

Catching a cold or the flu is impossible outdoors at the North Pole in winter. Winter temperatures are so low there that no known disease-causing microorganism can survive.

Quiz. Tourists in Holland can see, near Spaarndam lock, the statue erected to the famous little Dutch boy who held back the ocean and saved his city by putting his finger in the dike. What is peculiar about this monument to a legendary local hero? (Answer: page 29)

The War of Jenkins' Ear took place between England and Spain in 1739 after Captain Robert Jenkins indignantly displayed his severed ear, preserved in brine, before a parliamentary committee in London. Jenkins declared that while he was sailing in the West Indies a Spanish patrol had disfigured him.

"CAW!"

A recording of the alarm call of Pennsylvania crows was played for French crows. It caused them to gather rather than flee.

On December 10, 1903, the New York Times declared human flight to be a futile dream. The newspaper advised Samuel Langley, who was trying to develop a flying machine, to cease his efforts. "We hope," wrote the Times, "that Professor Langley will not put his substantial greatness as a scientist in further peril by continuing to waste his time, and the money involved, in further airship experiments. . . . For students and investigators of the Langley type there are more useful employments." One week after the newspaper appeared the Wright brothers made their first successful flight at Kitty Hawk.

The best way to bake fish is by the inch. Measure the fish at its widest point and bake it at 350 degrees, allowing five minutes for every half-inch of thickness.

One mark of his genius was that at his death, Leonardo da Vinci left notes with designs for the well digger, paddle wheel boat, sprocket chain, parachute, life jacket, helicopter, water turbine, steam gun, submarine, water pump, airplane, horseless carriage, and machine gun, and plans for mass production.

Marie Curie, codiscoverer of radium, was the first person known to have died of radiation poisoning. Until Curie's death it was not known that radiation was dangerous.

66 Sometimes when I look at my children I say to myself, 'Lillian, you should have stayed a virgin.' **99**
~Lillian Carter, mother of Jimmy and Billy

Quiz Answers

Page 19: Most people invent a theory like "atmospheric refraction," but the answer is much simpler and more remarkable. The rays don't diverge—they are still parallel up there in the sky, even though they don't look it. What you see is an illusion, like the railroad tracks that appear to get closer together in the distance. Where a pair of the sun's rays seem to be very far apart, they are actually much nearer to you than they are where the same rays appear to be closer together. The "Rays of Buddha" is a remarkable optical illusion because even when you know it's an illusion it is hard to get your brain to believe it. The rays still look as if they're spreading out, even though you know they're not.

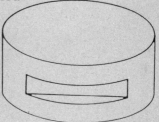

Page 20: There are several possible shapes that will produce the "front" and "side" views shown, but this is the simplest.

Page 21: True. He also wrote "The Charge of the Light Brigade," which became much more famous. The two poems describe incidents that occurred during the same battle.

Page 22: In South Africa. Japanese there are considered honorary Caucasians, which gives them the rights of "whites," while local Chinese there are still classified as "colored."

Page 25: Austin, Texas. (There are two Colorado Rivers in the United States.)

Page 27: The statue was erected in 1950 solely to satisfy American tourists who kept asking locals to show them the place where the little Dutch boy did his deed. The legend doesn't exist in Dutch folklore (and any smart local lad wouldn't plug a leak with a finger when he could use a stone). The tale of old Holland first appeared in Hans Brinker: or, The Silver Skates, a children's book by Mary Mapes Dodge, published in the United States in 1865. Americans accepted the story as Dutch, and visitors to the Netherlands kept asking the citizens of Haarlem to point out the famous dam. For years the Dutch decried the tale as a foreign fiction, but finally they gave in and built the "memorial statue" to provide an end to all the insistent inquiries, as well as a lucrative tourist attraction.

John James Audubon was able to paint birds like these barn owls in fine detail only by studying them closely. Most of his models were dead birds that he had shot. After he was through painting specimens, he often cooked and ate them. ~Photo courtesy of New-York Historical Society

CHAPTER 3

IT'S OK ... THEY'RE CRAZY

Thailand Television wanted to show reruns of "Laverne and Shirley," but recognized that it would be unacceptable in the Thai culture for unmarried young women to live away from their parents. To resolve the cultural conflict, the government television network began each episode with a statement that Laverne and Shirley had escaped from an insane asylum.

In London in 1763, William Cowper was so despondent that he decided to commit suicide. He hailed a cab and told the driver to take him to a bridge over the Thames, but the driver lost his way in dense fog. He told Cowper that he couldn't find the bridge or his way back to their starting point, and ordered him out of the cab. When he got out Cowper found himself in front of his own home. He went inside to write one of the most famous English hymns: "God Moves in a Mysterious Way His Wonders to Perform."

KEY PLAYER

Here's a trivia question guaranteed to give the most cocky sports fan a fit of head-scratching. Who played for the Brooklyn Dodgers, the New York Knicks, and the New York Rangers—three different teams in three different sports, all in the same season?

Answer: Gladys Gooding, the organist who provided music for all three New York teams in the forties and fifties.

HE'S SO FINED

In September 1976, George Harrison was convicted of copyright infringement and was ordered to pay $587,000. U.S. District Court Judge Richard Owen ruled that Harrison had taken the melody to his song "My Sweet Lord" from the 1963 Chiffons hit "He's So Fine." In a rare flight of judicial psychoanalysis Judge Owen opined that the former Beatle's plagiarism was probably unintentional: "His subconscious knew that song . . . but his conscious mind did not remember," he wrote. "It's a pain in the neck," Harrison said.

Quiz. What four-letter English word ends in "eny"? (Answer: page 43)

The door at 10 Downing Street, the residence of Britain's Prime Minister, opens only from the inside.

ROYAL EXCESSES

Anne Boleyn, condemned to death by her husband Henry VIII, had six toes on one foot, six fingers on one hand, and three breasts.

" No dog shall be in public without its master on a leash. "
~Belvedere, California, municipal ordinance

General Motors introduced its compact Chevy Nova to the Latin American market with an expensive promotion, but the car didn't sell. The company learned too late that in Spanish, **no va** means "it doesn't go."

When a researcher at the turn of the century published a paper on the mineral content of vegetables, he put a decimal point in the wrong place in his figure for the amount of iron in spinach. His error started a popular myth, the "Popeye theory," that spinach makes you strong because of its extremely high iron content. In fact, spinach has about the same amount of iron as other vegetables.

SALINE CHAPEL

The largest salt mine on earth is located in Zipaquirá, Colombia. The mine is so huge that it contains an entire cathedral with ceilings seventy-three feet high. The Salt Cathedral, as it is called, took six years to excavate and can seat almost five thousand worshipers.

66 This strange beating together of hands has no meaning. To me it is very disturbing. We try to make sounds like music, and then in between comes this strange sound you make. 99

~Leopold Stokowski, to an audience in 1929

Houses in Tokyo are numbered according to the order in which building permits were issued, and not by location or numerical sequence. It is said that finding a specific address is harder to do in Tokyo than in any other city in the world.

It's common knowledge that laborers in the Andes chew coca leaves to increase their strength and endurance. Less well known is that distances in the Peruvian Andes are measured in *cocadas* instead of kilometers. A *cocada* is the length of road a person can walk after chewing coca.

Whatzit Quiz

Here's another gadget. It's a plastic tube about two inches long. Its inner surface, covered with rough sandpaper, tapers from each end toward the tube's center. The tool might be found in a kitchen or a bar. Two words fully describe its use. What is it called? (Answer: page 43) ~Photo by Scot Morris

The diva was so world-renowned that another dish was also named after her—peach Melba, which consists of half a peach (poached in sweet syrup) served with ice cream, raspberry sauce, and whipped cream.

A few people in history are commemorated with eponyms—their names live on as words in the language. Nellie Melba is perhaps the only person doubly honored in this way. The toast of three continents who got her just deserts, Nellie is immortalized in the names of two foods, one a dieter's favorite, the other a high-calorie treat for those days of sweet indulgence.

~Photo courtesy of Culver Pictures

Helen ("Nellie") Porter Mitchell changed her name to Nellie Melba, in honor of her birthplace, Melbourne, Australia. She became one of the world's most celebrated opera singers—"the world's greatest soprano," some said—and during her forty-year career performed at London's Covent Garden and on the Continent, at New York's Metropolitan Opera, and in her native country. (She is shown here as Marguerite in Gounod's Faust.)

The story goes that the dieting Nellie ordered some toast at a London hotel but got slices that were dry and burnt. The maître d' apologized, but Dame Nellie said she liked the small, crisp pieces. The hotel started serving the thin-sliced bread regularly, and named it Melba toast in her honor.

ONE-DOWNMANSHIP

·{ When India presented the Soviet Union with a special gift—a needle with seven elephants carved into it—the Russians wanted to give an appropriate piece of micro-art in return. An Armenian artist named Edward Kazarian created the final work that the U.S.S.R. gave to India: a single polished human hair, hollowed out, with three hundred carved elephants inside.

❝ Nothing of importance happened today. ❞

~entry in the diary of King George III, July 4, 1776

THE BEST TOOLS FOR THE JOB

How do you remove a dangerous piece of metal from a dolphin's stomach without harming the 350-pound animal? California veterinarians faced with this problem came up with a remarkable solution. They called in professional basketball player Clifford Ray, of the Golden State Warriors, whose arms measured three feet, nine inches in length. Ray reached down the animal's gullet to its stomach, grasped the metal piece, and pulled it out safely.

Alaska's state flag was designed by a thirteen-year-old boy.

"IT SAYS HERE WE SHOULD HAVE TURNED LEFT AT BEATOSU"

The Michigan State Highway Commission map in 1979–80 included two towns—Goblu and Beatosu—that didn't exist. They had been slipped onto the map by a University of Michigan alumnus, and commemorated two rallying cries of the U of M football team, "Go Blue!" and "Beat OSU!" (Ohio State University). The names were removed from the 1980–81 map.

Tony Perkins lost his virginity to Victoria Principal.

Quiz. How high do you have to count before you'll use the letter a in the English spelling of a number name? (Answer: page 43)

PITY IN PARIS

Playwright Samuel Beckett was once stabbed by a pimp in a Paris street. He was found bleeding by the pianist Suzanne Deschevaux-Dumesnil. She visited him in the hospital, decided to live with him, and married him twenty-four years later.

The city's founder was Horace Wilcox, who acquired the land on which it now stands in 1888. Wilcox was a member of a temperance society and founded the city to serve as a model of sobriety, morality, and law and order. Only nondrinkers were allowed to settle there. For more than twenty years it was a peaceful place with no crime, no guns, no locked doors, and no jail. The city's name? Hollywood, California.

Salt was given to Roman soldiers as wages. That was their *salarium*, which is the origin of our word "salary."

At one time Frédéric Chopin wore a beard on one side of his face only. The pianist thought a full beard was unnecessary. "My audience sees only my right side," he explained.

ARACHNIDS SUCK

Spiders don't eat their victims—they drink them. The only way a spider can take nourishment is by sucking it through a mouth shaped like a soda straw. Spiders coat their prey with a fluid that causes it to dissolve—then they drink the victim for dinner.

Paul Cézanne taught his green parrot one phrase to speak over and over: "Cézanne is a great painter!"

"TURN IT DOWN!"

Surgeons, watchmakers, or others performing delicate manual tasks usually work in a quiet room and seem hypersensitive to noise. But they aren't just being temperamental. Studies in West Germany and at the University of Southampton in England have shown that unexpected noises can cause eye pupils to dilate. Because their dilating pupils are causing their eyes to lose focus and blur, people doing exacting work may be more bothered by noise than the rest of us.

The world's most active volcano is Hawaii's Mauna Loa, which has spewed enough lava to pave a four-lane highway going thirty times around the world. Much of Mauna Loa's lava was used to fertilize the farmland in Washington State's Cascade Range.

The state of Wyoming was named by a congressman from Ohio for a valley in Pennsylvania. The name was proposed by Representative James M. Ashley in 1865, to commemorate the Wyoming Valley in northeastern Pennsylvania, which was the site of a Revolutionary War massacre.

*I*ntrusive, celebrity-hounding photographers are called paparazzi, a word that sounds Italian but isn't. It comes from a character in a movie: the celebrity photographer Paparazzo in Federico Fellini's 1960 film, La Dolce Vita. Fellini chose the name, he said, because it sounded like "a buzzing, stinging, annoying sort of insect." ~Photo courtesy of Culver Pictures

Karl Marx was once a newspaper reporter for the New York Herald Tribune (then known as the Tribune). He worked in the paper's London office in 1849.

Quiz. The longest common word that can be typed out by using only the top row of letters on a standard typewriter (QWERT-YUIOP) has ten letters. What remarkable word is it? (Answer: page 43)

DEAR DIARY

❝ There will now be a short intermission while we bomb our target. ❞

~last entry in the log of *Enola Gay* co-pilot Robert A. Lewis before the atomic bomb was dropped on Hiroshima

The author of such novels about the rugged Old West as Riders of the Purple Sage and Code of the West, the man who created the literary genre the Western, was born with a most unrugged name: Pearl Grey. We can't blame him for dropping the "Pearl" when he decided to write professionally under the name Zane Grey.

Why is a drinking glass called a tumbler? The modern tumbler no longer tumbles, but it got its name from a Saxon device to encourage "chugging"—draining the entire contents at one draft, before setting the vessel down. The original drinking horn was unevenly weighted at the bottom so that it could not be set on a table without tumbling over and spilling its contents.

In 1850, Christian Sharps invented a rifle that was much easier to load than the flintlocks then carried by buffalo hunters. The rifle was so accurate that the inventor's name was commemorated in the term *sharpshooter*.

DEATHBED CONFESSION

"*All right, then, I'll say it. Dante makes me sick.***"**
    ~last words of Spanish playwright Lope de Vega

Every dog except the chow has a pink tongue: the chow's tongue is jet black. ~Photo courtesy of American Heritage Picture Collection

{The rasping, fiendishly husky voice of the little girl possessed by the devil in the 1973 movie *The Exorcist* was provided by Mercedes McCambridge, the actress who won an Academy Award for best supporting actress in *All the King's Men* in 1949.

{John Larroquette of TV's "Night Court" was the narrator of *The Texas Chainsaw Massacre*.

{The first person to go over Niagara Falls in a barrel was a woman. Anna Edson Taylor pulled off the stunt on October 24, 1901.

{No queen bee has ever stung a person. Queens use their stingers only on other queen bees. The queen's stinger isn't barbed as are those of other bees in the hive, so she's the only bee that can sting repeatedly without disemboweling herself.

{A quarter has 119 grooves on its circumference. How many grooves on a dime? Just one less—118.

CONTRARY TO OPINION . . .

{A plant does not *grow* toward light, it is *pushed* toward light. Light reduces the concentration of the growth hormone auxin on the bright side of the stem, so the dark side grows more rapidly, bending the stem toward the light.

{In Genesis 6 Noah is instructed by God to build an ark of gopher wood, 300 cubits long, 50 cubits wide, and 30 cubits high. A cubit was a unit of measurement based on a man's forearm—from the elbow to the tip of the middle finger—about 20 inches long. Thus, Noah's ark was a vessel 500 feet long, 83 feet wide, and 50 feet high.

{Adirondack Park, a state park in New York, is larger than any of the U.S. national parks.

{*Quiz.* Which state or states have boundaries that are formed only by straight lines? (Answer: page 43)

HIS OWN WORST OPPONENT

During the opening minutes of a wrestling match in Providence, Rhode Island, Stanley Pinto—normally a skilled professional wrestler—got himself entangled in the ropes. In his struggle to get free, he pinned his own shoulders to the mat for three seconds, untouched by his opponent, and was counted out.

William Gladstone and Benjamin Disraeli were bitter political enemies. After an angry debate in the House of Commons, Gladstone shouted to Disraeli, "Sir, you will come to your end either upon the gallows or of venereal disease!"

"I should say, Mr. Gladstone, that depends on whether I embrace your principles or your mistress," Disraeli replied.

THE NEWS CAME TOO LATE

In 1775, Lord North, Prime Minister of England under George III, proposed a number of conciliatory measures toward the American colonies to avoid a revolution. Parliament passed North's proposals, including giving the colonies the power to tax themselves and to set up their own civil administration and defense. But the news didn't reach America until five days after the Battle of Lexington. The Revolutionary War had already started.

THE PLOT ON HITLER'S HORMONES

The Office of Strategic Services planned an operation to feminize Adolf Hitler during World War II. The OSS tried to rob Hitler of his warrior's charisma for the German people by bribing his gardener to inject large amounts of estrogen into der Führer's carrots. "Hitler was close to the male-female line," wrote Stanley P. Lovell, who was director of research and development for the OSS, in his book Of Spies and Stratagems. "A push to the female side might make his mustache fall out and his voice become soprano."

The plot failed, Lovell says, either because Hitler's tasters detected something wrong with the veggies, or because the gardener simply threw the hormones away, pocketed the money, and double-crossed the OSS.

What's the fastest way to run in sand? A flat-footed stride has been found to work best, with neither the heel nor the toe touching the sand first and sinking the foot too deeply. The flat-footed running technique was developed by Australian lifeguards for their annual competitions.

Quiz· *Here's a curious crate created by Jerry Andrus, at right, who is recognized as one of the world's most creative magicians. Do you see anything wrong with it?*

Look carefully at the boards. The top front board, which Andrus holds in his left hand, appears to go behind a board at the back. And the bottom horizontal board at the back appears to pass on this side of one of the vertical boards in front. There is no trick photography here, and all the boards are straight and uncut.

How is the Impossible Box built? Try to sketch what it would look like viewed from another angle, before you turn to *page 43* *to see the truth of the matter.* ~Photo by Scot Morris

Quiz. *Which state or states have boundaries that are formed with no straight lines? (Answer: page 43)*

a desire to kill his father.

Hansen didn't collect, but his suit set a precedent that could change the nature of American family life forever.

THE MINISTER WHO CHANGED THE MONEY

During the Civil War, Treasury Secretary Salmon Chase received a moving letter from a clergyman who argued the tragic conflict was due to the religious backsliding in the land: "From my heart," he wrote, "I have felt our national shame in disowning God is not the least cause of our present national disorders." The letter impressed Chase, and prompted him to add the motto "In God We Trust" to all U.S. coins.

In the first lawsuit in the United States where a child sought damages from his own parents, Tom Hansen, twenty-four, of Boulder, Colorado, sued his parents for "psychological malparenting." Hansen wanted $350,000, claiming Mom and Pop were responsible for driving him crazy, which led to his frequent admissions to mental hospitals. He said that he filed the suit as an alternative to carrying out

In Siberia it can get so cold that the moisture in a person's breath freezes instead of forming vapor, and audibly falls to earth as ice crystals.

GREAT MOMENTS IN JOURNALISM

President John Quincy Adams once held an interview in the nude. Adams liked to skinny-dip in the Potomac on summer mornings, and once after his swim he found a reporter named Anne Newport Royall sitting on his clothes. Adams jumped back in the water and demanded that Miss Royall leave, but she refused to do so until he answered her questions about his pet project, the Bank of the United States. Adams had no choice but to grant the interview.

Redwood bark is fireproof, so fires in redwood forests burn inside the trees.

Quiz Answers

Page 32: Deny.

Page 33: Cork sharpener—for making it easier to recork wine bottles.

Page 35: One thousand. (Note: a number such as 101 is properly "one hundred one," not "one hundred and one.")

Page 37: Typewriter.

Page 39: Colorado, Wyoming, Utah.

Page 41: This picture tells it all. In fact, all the horizontal boards are in the same plane. On the left side, two boards stick out in front of the structure, on the right side, two boards jut out to the back. Everything was lined up for the camera, which was shooting with a telephoto lens from approximately 120 feet away.

Just to make it harder for you to get the "correct" visualization, the master illusionist added a master touch: the rope. The front rope appears to bend over the "top front" board, but actually the bend in the rope is three or four feet in front of the board. Andrus attached the bottom half of this rope to a thin wooden dowel to keep it stiff. The rope-and-pulley setting creates the final touch to the illusion that the crate is a solid, three-dimensional structure.   ~Photo by Scot Morris

Page 42: Hawaii.

Original print

By:

PRESENTED BY
MARIA G. CARR.
JULY, 1886.

Abraham Lincoln may have suffered from Marfan's syndrome, a hereditary disease that was first described over thirty years after Lincoln died. It wasn't until 1959 that a doctor linked the disease to the President, after discovering the syndrome in a child who shared a common ancestor with Lincoln. Symptoms of the illness include abnormally long arms and legs, asymmetry between the two sides of the body, disorders of vision, and heart problems, all of which were found in the President and/or his offspring. The California physician made the diagnosis of Marfan's syndrome from century-old photographs and health records of Lincoln and his family.   ~Photo by S. M. Fassett, courtesy of Chicago Historical Society

CHAPTER 4

James Garner received a Purple Heart award in 1983, the result of a wound he suffered in battle thirty-two years earlier in Korea. "I got it in the backside," Garner said. "I went into a foxhole headfirst, and I was a little late."

Long Beach, Miami Beach, Palm Beach—there are dozens of coastal resort cities with "Beach" in their names. But there's only one town in the United States named simply Beach. It's in landlocked North Dakota.

THE SHIP THAT SHOT ITSELF

In 1941 the British warship Trinidad sighted a German destroyer and fired a torpedo at it. The icy Arctic waters apparently affected the torpedo's steering mechanism—it began to curve in a slow arc. As the crew watched in horror, it continued curving slowly around until it was speeding right back at them at forty knots. The Trinidad's torpedo slammed into the Trinidad and caused so much damage it put the warship out of action for the rest of the war.

The Manhattan cocktail—whiskey and sweet vermouth, usually with a maraschino cherry—was invented by beautiful New York socialite Jennie Jerome. She later became Winston Churchill's mother.

The energy in ten minutes of one hurricane is equal to that of all the nuclear weapons in the world.

ACRONYM NATION

The country west of India was named by the British. They took the initials of Punjab, Afghanistan, and Kashmir, and added the ending stan, which means "land of," to create an Asian-sounding name: Pakistan.

Mr. Zig-Zag, whose visage is imprinted on every packet of a popular brand of "cigarette papers," and on the memories of millions who rolled something other than tobacco in those papers, was a real person. He was a Zouave, a man from Algeria who fought for the French army in the Crimean War.

THE GREEN FLASH

If you bite into a Wint-O-Green Life Saver in a dark place the candy will sparkle and your mouth will glow bluish-green. According to the research and development department at Life Savers, Inc., the phenomenon is produced when the bite releases energy from sugar crystals that causes methyl salicylate in the wintergreen flavoring to sparkle. Try it yourself, but remember that the flash is faint, so do your experimenting at night or in a dark closet.

In A Star Is Born a drunk asks Judy Garland to "sing 'Melancholy Baby.'" An extra played the drunk, but the voice was provided by Humphrey Bogart.

Think of Saudi Arabia and you might picture caravans of camels crossing the sand dunes. Would you believe the Saudis have to import both camels and sand? The camel population is declining in Arabia, so many animals have to be purchased from North Africa. As for the sand, there's plenty of it, but it's no good for making concrete. For building, Saudi Arabia must import tons of river sand all the way from Scotland.

G roucho Marx started wearing a false mustache in an early vaudeville act. One night, late for a performance, he quickly drew the mustache on with greasepaint. The audience didn't seem to notice, so he kept the trademark greasepaint mustache for the rest of his vaudeville career and through most of the Marx Brothers movies. Groucho didn't grow a real mustache as shown here (left) until he was well into middle age. ~Photos courtesy of Culver Pictures

Cats purr at twenty-five vibrations per second.   ~Photo by Carol Malcolm

Quiz· *There's a pattern to this progression of digits. Where in the sequence should the numeral "1" go? (Answer: page 59)*

8 5 4 9 7 6 3 2 0

THE STUPID SOLDIERS PROPOSAL

The problem with the military services, says Representative Les Aspin of Wisconsin, isn't that they're admitting too many dummies, "but too few." Aspin believes this results in intelligent men and women being assigned to simple jobs that bore them, lowering morale. The solution, Aspin proposed, is for the Pentagon to recruit more stupid people.

Ants don't sleep.

"TO DUST RETURNETH"

Where does the dust in your house come from? According to a study by London's Clinical Research Center, 70 percent of it consists of shed human skin.

In 1898 a Turkish wrestler named Yousouf Ishmaelo toured the United States and drew huge crowds. Ishmaelo didn't trust currency, so he converted his winner's purses into gold ingots and stashed them in a belt around his waist.

En route back to Turkey, Ishmaelo's ship, the *Burgoyne*, struck a reef and began to sink. Every passenger except the wrestler was rescued. The weight of the gold around his middle caused Ishmaelo to sink like a stone, and he drowned.

During World War II the U.S. Navy used world-champion chess player Reuben Fine to calculate probablities of where enemy subs might surface.

FOWL BALL RULE

Fenway Park, the home of the Boston Red Sox, has one of the most eccentric local ground rules in baseball: the pigeon-fly rule. If a batted ball hits one of the birds that have taken up permanent residence in the park, the ball is ruled dead.

AND THEY'RE OFF ... WAY OFF

The advent of the photo-finish camera took the guesswork out of judging horse races. It showed that human judges were generally accurate, but not on the close calls. In pre-camera 1935, judges called only 20 dead heats, but in 1938, when most tracks had cameras, films showed 264 dead heats. Apparently thousands of tied races had previously been miscalled due to human error and the desire to have a "decision."

An Arkansas law intending to limit pressure tactics in political campaigns was worded in such a way that it made voting virtually illegal. "No person," it said, "shall be permitted, under any pretext whatever, to come nearer than 50 feet of any door or window of any polling room, from the opening of the polls until the completion of the count and the certification of the counted returns."

Claude Monet's one-hundred-thousand-franc winnings in the French lottery of 1891 allowed him to quit his job and try his hand at what he really liked—painting.

GET YOUR JOB APPLICATION OFF TO A GOOD START

If you write a summary of your educational and professional experience, don't call it your "resume"—that's a mistaken word in fractured French. To spell it in correct French you will need two accent marks, one over each of the e's: "résumé." The English version of the word is "resume," with no accent marks whatsoever.

The Gunfight at the O.K. Corral may be part of Western lore, but it wasn't front-page news at the time. In the local Arizona newspaper, the Tombstone Epitaph, the legendary story was reported, under the headline THREE MEN HURLED INTO ETERNITY IN THE DURATION OF A MOMENT, starting on page three.

WORD ORIGIN

The word "decimate" doesn't mean to wipe out or exterminate, as many think. A clue to its derivation is the prefix "deci-," which means one tenth of something. Originally, the word described a bizarre punishment practiced on Roman soldiers. Disobedient legions would have every tenth man killed.

The U.S. Postal Service has assured diet-conscious customers that there is no more than one tenth of a calorie in the glue on the back of each postage stamp.

Alan Freed, the disc jockey who claimed that he coined the term "rock and roll" in 1951, was also a songwriter who penned two of Chuck Berry's biggest hits, "Maybelline" and "Nadine."

Marie-Augustin Marquis de Pélier made a serious mistake in 1786 when he whistled at Queen Marie Antionette as she was being escorted into a theater. He was arrested and spent the next fifty years in prison for his impertinence.

There's something about the sn sound that smells. A remarkable number of English words starting with those letters make reference to the nose—its appearance or function. Consider: snarl, sneer, sneeze, snicker, sniff, snivel, snob (one who turns the nose up), snoop (one who stick his nose into others' business), snoot, snore, snort, snot, snout, snub, and snuff. There's even a bird called the snipe (not related to the fictional bird of late-night initiations and "snipe hunts"), so named because of its prominent long bill.

WHEN JAPAN ATTACKED OREGON

It was widely believed that no enemy aircraft ever bombed the U.S. mainland. It isn't so, but the truth didn't come out until years after World War II. In September 1942, fires broke out in Oregon forests and were correctly blamed on the Japanese. The report went out that balloons launched in Japan equipped with firebombs had been carried to the United States on prevailing winds. In fact, the public was later told, a Japanese seaplane had crossed the U.S. western border and the pilot had dropped firebombs in an attempt to set the forests of the U.S. Northwest ablaze.

FINALLY, A *PRACTICAL* ROCKING CHAIR

W hen he looked at someone rocking in a rocking chair, Charles Singer of South Bend, Indiana, saw only wasted energy: all that motion, to no purpose. He decided to harness the latent power and invented this "Improved Rocking Chair," which uses the back-and-forth action of the chair to pump a bellows that blows air through a tube and back up to the chair's operator, to cool him down. Another energy-saving device produced by American know-how. Singer got his patent (No. 92,379) in 1869. ~Reproduced with permission from *Mousetraps and Muffling Cups* by Kenneth Lasson

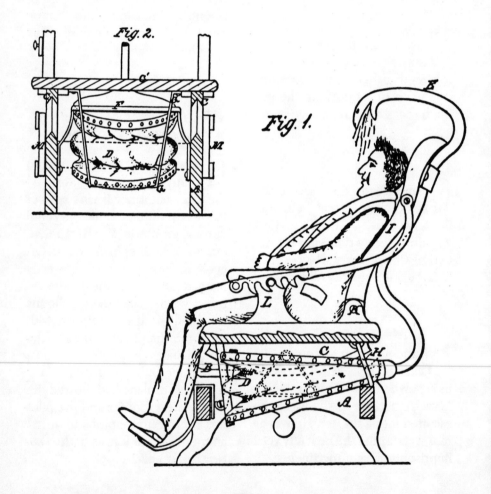

CIVIL WARFARE

In wartime, commerce between combatants usually comes to a halt. But during the Civil War a most unusual form of trade between the enemies was kept open. Abraham Lincoln was authorized to trade with the Confederacy in any way that would benefit the Union. The South had plenty of cotton for uniforms, but wanted opium to be used as a painkiller on wounded soldiers. The North had opium, but no cotton. Throughout the war there was a thriving trade of the North's opium for the South's cotton.

A female pigeon must be able to see another pigeon to lay eggs. Pigeon ovaries will not function if the bird is alone. But if she doesn't have company, her own reflection in a mirror will do nicely.

"A Japanese attack on Pearl Harbor is a strategic impossibility." That was the conclusion of Major George Fielding Eliot, a military science writer, in his article titled "The Impossible War with Japan." It appeared in *The American Mercury*, September 1938.

" The best time I ever had with Joan Crawford was when I pushed her down the stairs in *What Ever Happened to Baby Jane?* **"**
~Bette Davis

"Crocodile tears" is an expression based on fact. Crocodiles do produce tears, but they have nothing to do with emotion. They're glandular secretions to rid the crocodiles' eyes of excess salt.

In nearly every language around the world, the word for "mother" begins with an m sound.

Rudyard Kipling once gave an original manuscript to one of his children's nurses. "Take this script," the author said, "and some day if you are in need of money you may be able to sell it at a handsome price." Years later, in financial difficulty, the nurse did sell the manuscript of *The Jungle Book* and lived comfortably on the proceeds for the rest of her life.

Queen Victoria's doctors prescribed marijuana to relieve her menstrual cramps.

CRITICAL FAILURE

In 1836 a young woman wrote the eminent literary critic Robert Southey and enclosed an example of her work. If it wouldn't be too much trouble, the woman wrote, could Mr. Southey please give her an appraisal of her writing? Could she ever earn her living as a writer?

Southey's reply: "Literature cannot be the business of a woman's life, and it ought not to be. The more she is engaged in her proper duties, the less leisure she will have for it, even as an accomplishment and recreation. To those duties you have not been called, and when you are you will be less eager for celebrity."

Charlotte Brontë, author of *Jane Eyre*, was so devastated by Southey's reaction that she was unable to write at all for the next decade.

Several American cities founded by German immigrants changed their names as a result of World War I to avoid being associated with the enemy. Germantown, Texas, became Shroeder, after a young solider killed in battle. In 1918 Germantown, California, changed its name to Artois, after a region in northern France. Germantown, Kansas, became Mercier, after a Belgian religious leader. Potsdam, Missouri, changed its name to Pershing, to honor the American general. And the city fathers of Brandenburg, Texas, wanting to make their allegiance perfectly clear, named themselves after the flag. The name was changed to Old Glory in 1917.

DON'T WEAR BLACK TO A CHINESE FUNERAL

Black clothing symbolizes mourning in many parts of the world, but the association isn't universal. The preference in Iran is for brown (for withered leaves), in Syria it's blue (for heaven), and in China the appropriate mourning wear is white (for hope).

Quiz. Which is worth more, a pound of ten-dollar gold pieces or half a pound of twenty-dollar gold pieces, or are they worth the same? (Answer: page 59)

Emily Dickinson wrote more than eighteen hundred poems, only seven of which were published in her lifetime, and those without her consent.

{Rennet, used to curdle milk and make cheese, is an extract of the inner lining of a calf's fourth stomach.

LET'S GET SMALL

{In the nineteenth century, when miniature writing was in vogue, a Mr. Goldberg produced a legible page with fifty lines of print, each line less than a tenth of a millimeter high. It would take 87,500 of these pages to fill a square inch, the equivalent of fifty Bibles. Competition at the time was so keen that "Bibles per square inch" became a standard measurement of a miniaturist's skill.

The creator of Sherlock Holmes, Arthur Conan Doyle, was also an ophthalmologist.

{In 1789, when George Washington became President of the United States, there was a king of France, a Holy Roman Emperor who ruled much of Europe, a czarina in Russia, a shogun ruling Japan, and an emperor of China. Of all these powerful offices, only the presidency still exists.

{During the last months of World War I 20 million people died in a global influenza epidemic that spread from the battlefield trenches. The number of deaths caused by the flu was twice the number caused by the war.

Winston Churchill was a chronic snorer whose nighttime serenade was once measured at fifty-five decibels.

Quiz. What is the largest animal living today? What is the largest animal that ever lived on earth? (Answer: page 59)

OUT, DAMNED SPOT!

{Dogs do become locked in the sex act when the male's penis is captured by the contracted muscles of the vagina. *The Carpetbaggers* aside, however, and despite bawdy tales to the contrary, this trapped-penis syndrome is impossible in humans. There is no medical evidence of *penis captivus* ever occurring in human beings.

It is said that a man who serves as his own attorney has a fool for a client. In Oklahoma City a defendant in an armed robbery case decided to fire his lawyer and serve as his own counsel. Everything was going well until the store owner who had been robbed took the stand and identified the defendant, positively, as the man who did it. The defendant/lawyer argued with the owner, accused him of a faulty memory and of deliberately lying. Finally counsel lost his cool and shouted, "I should have blown your head off."

Thinking better of his statement, he quickly added, "If I'd been the one that was there."

The jury took only twenty minutes to bring in the verdict of guilty.

" I've had eighteen straight whiskeys. I think that's the record. **"**
~the last boast of poet Dylan Thomas, at his thirty-ninth birthday party, shortly before he died of alcoholism

"Cocos-de-mer" are the largest seeds on earth. They're found on palm trees on the Seychelles, islands off the east coast of Africa, weigh as much as fifty pounds each, and are bigger than basketballs. "Coco-de-mer" means coconut of the sea.

Ramree Island off the coast of Burma was the site of one of the bloodiest massacres of World War II, but it wasn't bullets or the usual weapons of war that did the killing. On the night of February 19, 1945, approximately one thousand retreating Japanese soldiers fled into a swamp to attempt to escape from encircling British forces. The Japanese were set upon by crocodiles—the animals had themselves taken refuge in the water to escape the din of battle—and only twenty men survived.

" For three days after death hair and fingernails continue to grow, but phone calls taper off. **"**
~Johnny Carson

TYPE CASTING

Cowboy star Tom Mix was a U.S. marshal before he acted in Western movies.

Quiz. Which is heavier—a cup of skim milk, a cup of whole milk, or a cup of cream? (Answer: page 59)

S amuel F. B. Morse didn't turn his attention to science until he was in his forties
and after he had won wide acclaim as an artist. The inventor studied art at Yale.
He became internationally known as a portrait painter, and won a gold medal from
the English Adelphi Society for his still lifes. Morse's portrait of the Marquis de
Lafayette still hangs in New York's City Hall. (Shown here is The Muse, a portrait
from about 1836 of his daughter, Susan Walker Morse.) ~Photo courtesy of The
Metropolitan Museum of Art, bequest of Herbert L. Pratt, 1945

efore the Spanish conquest in 1532, the Incas ruled an enormous empire in South America from Ecuador to Chile. Even so, at no time in their history did such "basic" ideas as the wheel, the arch, or writing occur to them.

MOUNTAIN MAMA

If you look at a mountain range and are reminded of parts of a woman's anatomy, you aren't alone. A pair of mountains in Alaska are officially known as the Jane Russell Peaks. And where do you think the Tetons, in the Grand Teton National Park in Wyoming (above), got their name? Not from crude American slang, as you might think, but from the same imagery nonetheless. The name comes from the French word for a woman's breast, téton. ~Photo courtesy of Grand Teton National Park

Quiz Answers

Page 49: The numbers are in alphabetical order, according to the way they are spelled. "One" should go between "nine" and "seven."

Page 50: Ten times (not eleven, as most people think). If you doubt it, try the experiment with a real watch.

Page 54: A pound is worth twice as much as half a pound.

Page 55: The answer to both questions is the same: the sulphur-bottom whale, which can weigh over one hundred and fifty tons.

Page 56: The skim milk is heaviest, cream is lightest. (Did you forget that cream floats on top of milk?)

CHAPTER 5

Douglas Corrigan, a thirty-one-year-old airplane mechanic, filed for clearance in July 1938 to fly solo across the Atlantic, but authorities turned him down because his plane failed a safety inspection, had no radio and no beam finder. He took off from Floyd Bennett Field in New York, supposedly for his home in California.

The next day he landed in Dublin, Ireland. He claimed that his compass had broken and that, flying in a heavy fog, he had had to guess the direction to California. When he landed, he said he had no idea where he was. And when told he was thousands of miles east of his "intended" destination, he said only, "I guess I flew the wrong way." Back in the States he became a popular hero, got a tickertape parade down Broadway, made a movie about his "accidental" flight, and was known from then on by the nickname "Wrong Way" Corrigan.

Years later, in the seventies, Wrong Way was asked once again whether he had really intended to fly to California. "Sure," he said. "Well, at least I've told that story so many times that I believe it myself now." ~Photo courtesy of Culver Pictures

TRAGIC TYPO

On July 22, 1962, the Mariner I space probe was launched from Cape Canaveral, Florida, programmed to provide the first close-up view of the planet Venus. It fell into the Atlantic four minutes after lift-off, an $18.5 million loss for the U.S. space program. An investigation later revealed the cause of the disaster—a single minus sign had been mistakenly omitted from the instructions punched into the rocket's computer.

In the movie *The Ten Command-ments*, as Moses descends from the mountain, the man who drums, standing with his back to the camera, is Herb Alpert.

The penguin is the only bird in the world that can swim but cannot fly.

A major reason Washington's army starved at Valley Forge was greed: Pennsylvania farmers preferred to sell their crops to the British for cash rather than give them away to hungry American soldiers.

FASTER THAN A SPEEDING CHICKEN

Why did the National Research Council of Canada develop a cannon that fires dead chickens at speeds up to 620 m.p.h? To test air-plane parts to see whether they could withstand mid-air collisions with birds. The pneumatic gun is equipped to fire either a standard four-pound chicken (for testing windshields), or a jumbo eight-pounder for testing the tails—of the airplanes, that is.

THE STALL OF FAME

"This room was honored by the presence of Jacqueline Bouvier Kennedy Onassis on the occasion of the wedding of Joseph P. Kennedy II and Sheila B. Rauch, February 3, 1979." This commem-orative plaque is in the ladies' rest room at Ray Utz's Arco gas station, where Mrs. Onassis stopped, briefly, on her way to Gladwyne, Pennsylvania, for the wedding of her nephew (Robert Kennedy's oldest son).

Nine pennies weigh one ounce. That rule of thumb can come in handy if you want to check the accuracy of a postage scale.

Teachers may be unconsciously prejudiced by names. In San Diego, eighty elementary school teachers were asked to grade eight essays of similar quality, submitted under false names. The teachers awarded higher grades to an essay if it was supposedly written by a David, Michael, Karen, or Lisa. The same essays got lower grades if the student's name attached was Elmer, Hubert, Adelle, or Bertha.

A HANDY I.D.

{Treasury Secretary Michael Blumenthal found himself in an embarrassing situation in Beethoven's, an expensive San Francisco restaurant in 1979. Blumenthal was confronted with a sizable dinner bill, an expired Visa card, and a waiter who wanted proof of signature to back up an out-of-town check. Blumenthal solved his predicament in a way only he could: he produced a dollar bill and pointed out his own signature, *W. M. Blumenthal*, in the bottom right-hand corner. The signatures matched, and Blumenthal's personal check was accepted.

Turkeys aren't known for their intelligence. Newborn turkeys have to learn how to eat or they'll starve to death. Farmers put seed on the floor where the fledgling turkeys walk, hoping the chicks will peck at it and catch on. Turkeys caught in the rain have been known to look up and hold their mouths open so long that they die by drowning. ~Photo by F. Overton, courtesy of Department of Library Services, American Museum of Natural History

Quiz· Only one radio station in the United States spells out the name of the city from which it broadcasts. What are its call letters? (Answer: page 75)

{What's the most effective way to give a tree a drink? Pouring all the water at the base is the worst way. The roots that absorb water are usually away from the base, mostly in a circle in the soil that is just beyond the tree's outermost branches.

PRINCE PRINTS

Breeders and trainers take nose prints from dogs and keep them on file for identification purposes. Nose prints have been found to be more distinctive than paw prints. A dog's nose print is as individual for each dog as the fingerprint is for humans.

Ivanhoe, Minnesota calls itself "The Story Book Town." And for good reason. In the 1820s when the man representing the Western Town Lot company was plotting a new village in Lincoln County, he passed the time reading a novel by Sir Walter Scott. The book impressed him so much that he not only named the village after it, *Ivanhoe*, but named all the streets after names in the book: George, Bruce, Rowena, Saxon, Rotherwood, Wallace, Rebecca, Huber, Sherwood, Norman, and Harold.

IN NEBULOSITY WE TRUST

The state motto of New Mexico is *Crescit Eundo*, which means "It Grows as It Goes." The state motto of Washington is *Alki*, Chinook Indian for "By and By."

When beekeeper A. I. Root of Medina, Ohio, read an obscure notice in a Dayton newspaper on the Wright brothers' first motorized flight, he realized its historical importance, wrote a full report on it, and sent it to the *Scientific American*. The august science magazine rejected his article, so Root submitted it to another journal, which accepted it. The first published report on man's first powered flight appeared in *Gleanings in Bee Culture*.

TRUCE AT LAST

World War I lasted forty-four years for Andorra. The tiny republic in the Pyrenees played such a minor role in the war that the Allies didn't invite it to the Versailles Peace Conference. As a result, Andorra didn't formally make peace with Germany until 1958.

Novelist Nathanael West died within twenty-four hours of his friend F. Scott Fitzgerald. West was killed in a car crash while driving to Los Angeles for Fitzgerald's funeral.

Florence Nightingale was a nurse to wounded soldiers for only two years. The founder of the nursing profession was stricken with fever during her service in the Crimean War and spent her last fifty years as an invalid.

❝ *I can't mate in captivity.* **❞**
~Gloria Steinem, on why she never married

64

DESTINED FOR STARDOM?

·{Shirley MacLaine claims to have been named after Shirley Temple.

Quiz· What's the largest organ in the human body? And what's the largest muscle in the human body? (Answers: page 75)

{"Dear Sir," a San Diego subscriber wrote *The Village Voice*, "as one of your earliest subscribers, I feel I am entitled to challenge you to run this letter without one of your cutesie-pie headlines."

The Village Voice was equal to the challenge. The letter was printed under the headline: FUCK YOU

{"I'm sorry, Mr. Kipling, but you just don't know how to use the English language. This isn't a kindergarten for amateur writers." So read the pink slip that fired Rudyard Kipling from his reporting job on the *San Francisco Examiner*. At the time, Kipling had already written his classic, *The Man Who Would Be King*.

{Singer Rudy Vallee lived on Pyramid Place in Hollywood. He lobbied the city to change the name of the street but other residents objected and his request was denied. The crooner wanted the road renamed in his own honor, *Rue de Vallee*.

THANKS, TOM

{As if the electric light, the phonograph, and the motion-picture camera weren't enough, Thomas Edison invented the following, too: wax paper, the mimeograph machine, the dictating machine, a variety of Portland cement, an electric vote recorder, the chemical phenol, an electric pen, and a version of the stock ticker. He also gave us the light socket and light switch, and when he died he was working on a machine that, in his words, was "so sensitive that if there is life after death, it will pick up the evidence."

·{An Egyptian papyrus from 1850 B.C. is the earliest record of planned parenthood. A prescribed mixture of honey, soda, and crocodile excrement was to be placed in the vagina to act as a contraceptive.

Lake Superior, covering almost thirty-two thousand square miles, is the largest freshwater lake in the world. But the world's *biggest* freshwater lake, surprisingly, is Lake Baikal in Siberia. Even though its surface takes up less than twelve thousand square miles, it is over a mile deep in places, and has more water volume than any other lake. Lake Baikal accounts for one fifth of all the volume of all the freshwater lakes in the world.

Elias Howe, who for years had been trying to invent a practical sewing machine, fell asleep one night and had a nightmare. He dreamed that primitive tribesmen had captured him and were threatening to run him through with their spears. Howe noticed that the natives' spears all had holes through them at their pointed ends. When he suddenly awoke he realized the idea that would lead to a perfected sewing machine: use a needle with a hole not through its base or middle but through its tip.

IN THE GROOVE

In 1933, in a bowling exhibition at Olney Alleys in Philadelphia, professional bowler Bill Knox bowled a perfect game—twelve strikes in a row—without ever seeing the pins. Knox had a special screen built, and he enlisted two pin boys to hold it about a foot above the foul line so that it blocked his view not only of the pins but of most of the alley as well. He did it to demonstrate the technique of "spot" bowling, or releasing the ball at a chosen point on the lane. The audience in the stands could see around the screen and watched in amazement as Knox toppled all the pins on twelve consecutive rolls—scoring a perfect game without ever seeing what he was aiming at.

In 1977, Chuck Ross, a writer frustrated by his inability to find a publisher, tried an experiment to prove something to himself. He typed up a manuscript copy of Jerzy Kosinski's novel *Steps*, which had won the National Book Award for fiction in 1969, and submitted it to fourteen publishers under his own name. Each of them rejected the manuscript—including Random House, the novel's original publisher.

The test struck a blow for all unpublished writers' self-esteem. If a publisher could reject an acclaimed novel it had already published, how seriously could any writer take those inevitable "rejection slips"?

❝ I am sitting in the smallest room in the house. I have your review in front of me. Soon it will be behind me. **❞**

~Max Reger, to a music critic

ONE-BITE LAW

In Colorado Springs, a law says that every dog has the right to one bite.

IN AND OUT OF A JOB

In 1978, William Smith of Waukegan, Illinois, was elected Lake County Auditor. But in a referendum on the same ballot, voters abolished the position of auditor altogether. "I feel like I've gone off a diving board and suddenly found the pool was empty," Smith said.

Lon Chaney's son, Creighton Chaney, was a failed songwriter. He changed his name to Lon Chaney, Jr., and became a horror-movie star, most memorably as the Wolf Man in 1941 (here, at left, with Bela Lugosi). Lon Sr. died of throat cancer in 1930. Lon Jr. died of throat cancer in 1973. ~Photo courtesy of Culver Pictures

TRYING TO SIMPLIFY THINGS

{The state of Kansas once passed a law rounding off the value of pi from 3.14159265 ... to an even 3.

Quiz. The Duke of Beaufort learned a game called "poona" in India late in the nineteenth century. When he brought the game back home he found that Englishmen wouldn't play a game named "poona," so he searched around for a more refined-sounding name, and finally picked the name of his estate in Somerset. What was the new name chosen for the Indian game of poona? (Answer: page 75)

ONLY A GAME

On June 27, 1969, a war between El Salvador and Honduras was started by a soccer game. The neighboring countries were opponents in a World Cup tie-breaker when a referee awarded a late penalty kick to El Salvador. El Salvador scored on the kick, won the game 3–2, and won the match.

When word of the referee's call spread through both capital cities, riots broke out as fans refought the decision with opposition supporters. On July 3, as a result of the riots, the countries declared war on each other. Result? Two thousand soldiers died and the Central American Common Market was disbanded, causing food shortages and starvation in both countries. Incidentally, El Salvador lost its next game and was eliminated from the World Cup tournament.

66 It is now quite lawful for a Catholic woman to avoid pregnancy by a resort to mathematics, though she is still forbidden to resort to physics or chemistry. 99
~H. L. Mencken (1880–1956)

A pound of shelled walnuts contains as many calories as a pound of butter and as much fat as a pound of bacon.

{The 1963 recording of the rock song "Louie Louie," by the Kingsmen, was banned from air play on several radio stations because of the widespread belief that the song's lyrics were dirty. Rumors spread that the words included such lines as "Tell her I'll never lay her again," "I shoot a wad into her hair," and "I fuck a girl endlessly." An FCC investigation failed to squelch the story. The song had actually been written six years earlier, but when the Kingsmen recorded their version singer Lynn Easton mumbled the words so thoroughly that listeners had to use their imaginations to decide what they were.

The writer, Richard Berry, says the song is a sailor's lament, as spoken to a bartender named Louie, and that the Kingsmen singer didn't change the words in the studio—he just slurred them so badly that people gave them their own interpretations. Thus was the legend born. Here are the "real" lyrics, as reported by Cecil Adams in his book *The Straight Dope*:

"Louie Louie, me gotta go. Louie Louie, me gotta go. A fine little girl, she wait for me. Me catch the ship across the sea. I sailed the ship all alone. I never think I'll make it home. Louie Louie, me gotta go. Three nights and days we sailed the sea. Me think of girl constantly. On the ship, I dream she there. I smell the rose in her hair. Louie Louie, me gotta go. Me see Jamaican moon above. It won't be long me see me love. Me take her in my arms and then I tell her I never leave again. Louie Louie, me gotta go."

(By Richard Berry, Copyright © 1957–1963 by Limax Music Inc.)

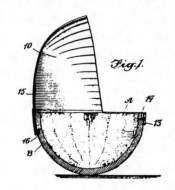

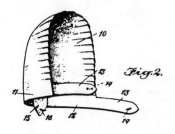

AN END TO OFFENSIVE GRAPEFRUIT

Joseph Fallek of Brooklyn, New York, was squirted in the eye with grapefruit juice once too often. He designed this shield, which everyone at his breakfast table was required to use when eating grapefruit. It prevented juice-spattering accidents. Fallek got U.S. Patent No. 1,661,036 for his device, on February 28, 1928. ~Reproduced with permission from *Mousetraps and Muffling Cups* by Kenneth Lasson

Quiz. What is the only game in which the ball is always in the possession of the team on defense, and the offensive team can score without touching the ball? (Answer: page 75)

Since rodents' teeth never stop growing, the animals have to gnaw constantly to grind them down.

Garlic rubbed on the soles of your feet will be noticeable on your breath within one hour.

While artists in ancient China often depicted genitalia and copulating couples, it was strictly taboo to show a naked female foot.

❝ I figure you have the same chance of winning the lottery whether you play or not. **❞**
~Fran Lebowitz

In 1945 the famous caricaturist, Al Hirschfeld, put the name of his new-born daughter, Nina, into his drawing for the musical Are You with It? Since then, Hirschfeld has regularly hidden NINAs in his stylized drawings, and finding the NINAs has been a ritual game for his fans reading the drama page of the Sunday New York Times.

Hirschfeld has occasionally considered dropping the practice, but, as he has written, "unfortunately I do not have the resources ('guts' may be the more apt word) to put an end to it. The first intimation that I had created a Frankenstein 'indestructible' was the incredible response I received the first time I deliberately left Nina's name out of a drawing. Mail descended on me from all over, demanding, 'Where is it?' 'My wife says it's here in the feathers.' 'Our weekly pool cannot pay off without verification from you.' 'Is this it?' "

Hirschfeld once acceded to his daughter's request to put the name of her girlfriend, Liza, into a drawing. This was an "unpardonable error," the artist later said. "All hell broke loose. . . . Flowers and telegrams arrived, one all the way from Alaska, congratulating my wife and me on the new arrival." Since 1960 Hirschfeld has, as an argument-settling device, appended a number next to his own signature indicating the number of NINAs in the drawing (facing page).

Some fans take Hirschfeld's work as more than just a game. The U.S. Air Force has used NINA-searches as an exercise to train bomber pilots to spot targets, and a Pentagon consultant has scanned Hirschfeld drawings as part of a $60,000 grant for the study of different techniques of camouflage.

Quiz: Can you find the three NINAs in this depiction of the Marx Brothers? Answer: page 75

~© 1989 Al Hirschfeld. Drawing reproduced by special arrangement with Hirschfeld's exclusive representative, the Margo Feiden Galleries, New York

THEY'VE GOT YOUR NUMBER

Your Social Security number is a code that tells some vital information about you. Here is what the numbers mean:

The first three digits identify the state in which you lived when you first registered. The states are numbered roughly from east to west. Numbers 001 to 003 are for people from New Hampshire, for example. Numbers 050 to 134 are for New Yorkers, 362 to 383 for Michigan folks, and 521 to 524 designate residents of Colorado.

The next two numbers are in code and identify the year you applied. Generally, the higher the number the more recently it was issued.

The last four digits are assigned at random and, taken with the others, are your citizen's identification number permanently on file with the U.S. Government.

A SWEET'S START

Laws were passed in Illinois in the 1880s prohibiting the sale of ice-cream sodas on Sunday. Some soda fountain owners got around the law by omitting the soda water and serving only the ice cream and syrup. They called their dodge a "Sunday soda," later shortened to "Sunday" before it became "sundae."

More Irish live in New York City than in Dublin, more Italians than in Rome, and more Jews than in Tel Aviv. The city also has the highest population of blacks in the world—second place going to Kinshasa, Zaire.

Isaac Newton dropped out of school as a teenager at his mother's urging. She wanted him to take up farming.

Whatzit Quiz

Here's a plastic kitchen tool about the size of a measuring spoon. What is it? (Answer: page 75) ~Photo by Scot Morris

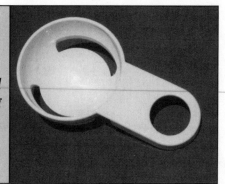

Ulysses Simpson Grant was not the President's real name. He was born Hiram Ulysses Grant. Where did the Simpson come from? From a mistake in a letter recommending Grant for admission to West Point. Grant's congressman thought the young man's first name was Ulysses and guessed that his middle name must be his mother's maiden name, Simpson. Hiram decided he liked being called Ulysses Simpson Grant— perhaps it was those patriotic initials—and so he used the name from then on.

Robert Chesebrough invented petroleum jelly. He lived to the age of ninety-six and attributed his longevity to the fact that he swallowed a spoonful of the stuff every day from the age of twenty-two, when he first concocted it, until his death. When he was thirty-eight, he introduced the product to the public under the name Vaseline.

The single most popular size in women's shoes is 7½ B, accounting for almost 7 percent of all shoe sales.

Quiz. What is the only state that shares no letters in common with its own capital? (Answer: page 75)

In 1949, Edward A. Murphy was an engineer at the Wright Field Aircraft Lab in Ohio. When a gauge he designed wouldn't work, Murphy traced the problem to improper wiring by a technician. "If there's a way to do it wrong, he will," Murphy said. The remark, repeated and modified over time, was to become the pessimist's favorite challenge to order in the universe, Murphy's Law: "If anything can go wrong, it will."

On April 1, 1966, the BBC broadcast a TV documentary on spaghetti-growing in Italy, complete with film of farmers picking market-ready strands of spaghetti from the vine. The documentary was supposed to be an April Fools' Day joke, but it caused no comment whatsoever as the vast majority of British viewers accepted the news that Italy's "pasta farmers" had managed to overcome the ravages of the "spaghetti weevil, which has been especially destructive in recent years."

DON'T SNIFF THE CORK

When a sommelier hands you the cork from an expensive wine bottle you have just ordered, whatever you do, don't sniff it or you'll reveal your wine ignorance. As wine expert Raymond Wellington says, "It's the wine itself you want to smell. After all, a cork smells like a cork."

What you are expected to do during this little ritual is to examine the cork closely to assure yourself that it is genuine and in good condition. An authentic cork has been put in the bottle at the winery. If the wine is French, the cork should be stamped "*Mis en bouteille dans nos caves.*" The cork should be moist, indicating that the wine was stored properly, on its side, so that the cork always remains wet and expanded to block the entry of air. A dry or crumbly cork may indicate that air has reached the wine and ruined it.

So look at the cork and feel it, but resist the temptation to smell. The only bad wine you'll detect with a cork-sniff is one that has already turned to vinegar, and you'll smell that more readily in the wine itself.

Goat's milk is naturally homogenized.

On April 2, 1868, a Hawaiian named Holua saved his own life by surfing a 50-foot-tall tidal wave to shore. According to files at the Bernice P. Bishop museum in Honolulu, Holua was carried to sea when his house was ripped from its foundations as a series of tidal waves hit the south shore of the island of Hawaii. Holua tore a plank from his disintegrating house and used it to ride the next tidal wave safely to the beach at Punaluu. Most surfing experts consider waves of more than 35 feet not to be ridable.

Cats purr while both inhaling and exhaling, but with different vocal cords.

There are Japanese who fish with cormorants instead of nets or hooks and lines. Cormorants are large birds with pelican-like pouches beneath their beaks. The fishermen let the birds fly out on leashes to dive for fish. The cormorants don't give up their catches voluntarily, of course. Iron rings around their necks prevent them from swallowing the day's catch.

Quiz Answers

Page 63: WACO.

Page 65: The skin is the largest organ; the buttock is the largest muscle.

Page 68: Badminton.

Page 70: Baseball.

Page 71: The three NINAs are in Groucho's right sleeve, in the folds of Chico's music box, and in the curls of Harpo's hair.

Page 72: Egg separator. Crack an egg and plop the innards into this spoon. The white drains through the slots while the yolk stays in the center.

Page 73: South Dakota. Its capital is Pierre.

TRENDSETTER

When Queen Elizabeth I of England lost her hair from smallpox at the age of twenty-nine, she started wearing wigs. Wigs became the fashion rage of Europe, a style that lasted for centuries. ~Photo courtesy of American Heritage Picture Collection

CHAPTER

6

A pigeon's feathers weigh more than its bones.

THE SWEETENER WAS TOO SHARP

Henry Ford once observed sugar crystals under a microscope and then refused to eat granulated sugar for the rest of his life. He thought it might slice up his internal organs.

The World Trade Center in New York has so many offices that it qualifies for its own zip codes—10047 and 10048.

The first person ever to belch on national radio was Melvin H. Purvis, head of the Chicago office of the FBI. Purvis was the guest on a show sponsored by Fleischmann's Yeast, in 1935, and in the middle of reading a commercial the famed "G-man" emitted a loud burp. For many years thereafter Fleishmann's Yeast was nicknamed "Purvis' Folly."

It's too early for a Polish pope.
~Polish cardinal Karol Wojtyla on October 14, 1978, three days before being elected Pope. He took the name John Paul II.

H. G. Wells imagined a new kind of weapon in his 1914 story "The World Set Free." He called the fictional device an "atomic bomb."

The song with the longest title was written in 1941: "I'm Looking for a Guy Who Plays Alto and Baritone and Doubles on a Clarinet and Wears a Size Thirty-Seven Suit." It was a hit, too.

Quiz. What fruit has its seeds on the outside? (Answer: page 93)

The streets are safe; it's only the people who make them unsafe.
~Frank Rizzo, former mayor of Philadelphia

In March of 1949, Popular Mechanics magazine looked as far into the future as it dared, and wrote this about the future of computing: "Where a calculator on the ENIAC is equipped with 18,000 vacuum tubes and weighs 30 tons, computers in the future may have only 1,000 vacuum tubes and perhaps only weigh 1½ tons."

BUG WITH A BOILER

The bombardier beetle has a very effective way to defend itself. When attacked or disturbed, the insect squirts jets of hot acid to burn its antagonist. This acid is formed by chemicals secreted by two glands into a reservoir inside the beetle's body. The sudden mixture of these chemicals causes a reaction that heats the liquid as high as the boiling point of water, but it's a mystery why the scalding liquid does no harm to the beetle itself.

NERVY CONTESTANT

A man who called himself Patrick Quinn won $58,600 on the NBC game show "Super Password," the largest prize in the show's history. The man was using an alias. A viewer recognized him as Kerry Ketchem, a fugitive in an insurance fraud case, and alerted authorities. When Ketchem showed up to collect his winnings federal agents were there to arrest him and see that he was sent to jail.

Before 1859 baseball umpires were comfortably seated in padded rocking chairs behind home plate.

Quiz· *In many liquor stores you can buy pear brandy with a real pear inside the bottle, The pear is whole and ripe. How did it get inside?*

In trying to answer this, some people think the bottle has been cut, either up the sides or at the base, but it hasn't. The bottle is genuine. Some think the bottle's neck was heated until it expanded enough to let the pear in, then it cooled and contracted; but glass that hot would surely scorch any piece of fruit that came near it. Some speculate that the pear was dehydrated and dropped inside, where it resumed its shape after soaking in brandy. But a dehydrated pear doesn't turn into a ripe pear when placed in liquid: it becomes a wet dehydrated pear.

If none of those answers are correct, how did the pear get in the bottle? (Answer: page 93) ~Photo by Scot Morris

A TRANQUIL TOWN

·{Lithium is a metallic salt used to treat manic depressives. Biochemists from the University of Texas have discovered surprising amounts of natural lithium occurring in the water supply of El Paso, which they believe might account for the fact that El Paso has one of the nation's lowest rates of admission to mental hospitals.

Bothered by mosquitoes? Check what you're wearing. Mosquitoes are twice as attracted to the color blue as to any other color.

Glen Campbell once sang backup with the Beach Boys.

He was "a complete ham," said band leader Xavier Cugat about the Hollywood extra who appeared in such films as *Bathing Beauty* with Esther Williams. "He was a young, ambitious, attractive boy . . . and he had aspirations for being discovered. He was a typical Latin looker, so he was in quite a lot of crowd scenes in those big, splashy films set against a Latin background." The man eventually left the movies and took his ambitions and aspirations back to the country where he and Cugat had both grown up—Cuba—where he led a revolution. The film extra's name: Fidel Castro.

THE PEDANT AND THE POET

Charles Babbage, the British mathematician who invented the calculating machine that led to the modern computer, was a stickler for accuracy. He once wrote a letter to Lord Tennyson about the poet's line, "Every moment dies a man/Every moment one is born." Babbage wrote: "It must be manifest that if this were true, the population of the world would be at a standstill."

Clearly, Tennyson was wrong. Babbage's recommended change: "Every moment dies a man/Every moment 1¹⁄₁₆ is born."

OOPS

Not many details are known about the medical malpractice suit filed by Harold Michael, but it is reported that he was awarded $825,000. The judge in the common pleas court of Allegheny County, Pennsylvania, refused to discuss the case, saying, "This matter is just too sensitive."

A doctor who operated on Michael, four months before the twenty-six-year-old was to be married, accidentally amputated the man's penis.

On a clear, moonless night and when there are no obstructions, the human eye can see the light of a single match as far as fifty miles away.

A Potawatomi Indian brave bet that he could run to a distant river and back before a pot of water set on a fire came to a boil. He won the bet, and the Indians commemorated the feat in their name for the valley where they lived in what is now the state of Michigan. They called the valley *Ke-ke-kala-kala-mazoo*, which means "where the water boils in the pot." White settlers shortened the name to Kalamazoo.

HOW AMERICA SAVED COLUMBUS' LIFE

{The debate over Columbus' voyage in Queen Isabella's court had nothing to do with whether the earth was round or flat. The earth was known to be round then, the question was, how round? Columbus' opponents said that he had underestimated the earth's size and that it would be impossible to sail west from Europe to reach India before his supplies ran out. We now know they were right. The voyage would have been doomed if an unknown continent hadn't been where it was to save Columbus and his crews.

Quiz. The eight letters in the word pictures can be transposed into only one other English word. What is it? (Answer: page 93)

{You are tallest in the morning. Your height may increase by as much as a third of an inch while you sleep. The sponge-like discs between your vertebrae are filled with liquid. During your waking hours this liquid is squeezed out from between the stacked discs. While you sleep it's reabsorbed.

{Natural gas has no smell. The unpleasant odor is added artificially as a safety precaution so that people can detect gas leaks and will be motivated to stop them immediately.

{The bowie knife, with its guard plate between the heavy blade and the handle, was not invented by Jim Bowie, the heroic defender of the Alamo. It was invented by Rezin Pleasant Bowie, Jim's lesser-known brother.

{Joseph Priestly is famous for discovering oxygen in 1774. Less well known is the fact that he discovered how to make carbonated water—he's the Father of Soda Pop. He also found that a gooey substance would erase pencil marks on paper. Since he used it by rubbing it across the marks, he called the stuff "rubber."

{A prize for Euphemism of the Year was once awarded by the *New York Times* to the Central Intelligence Agency, which had designated one of its assassination teams as a "health alteration committee."

ACCIDENTAL VEGETABLE

Food critic James Beard described the Belgian endive as "one of the most delectable and delicate vegetables in the Western world." In 1843 a gardener in Belgium inadvertently left a bunch of chicory nuts in a damp, dark cellar. In the absence of sunshine, the roots sprouted fine white leaves that no one had ever seen (or tasted) before. The new vegetable was a winner. The Belgian endive, the one James Beard called "absolutely delicious" and "the magical vegetable," originated in a mistake.

❝ *Television—a medium. So called because it is neither rare nor well done.* **❞**
~Ernie Kovacs

RHYME AND REASON

"Old King Cole" from the nursery rhyme was an actual monarch who ruled Britain around 200 A.D. The king was said to be "a jolly old soul" much beloved by his subjects, and also very fond of music—"he called for his fiddlers three."

History shows that Jack Horner really existed, too. An emissary from the bishop of Glastonbury, he was to deliver some deeds of title to King Henry VIII, and hid the extremely valuable documents in an innocent-looking Christmas pie. Supposedly during the trip Horner stole a deed to a private estate, thus helping himself to a "plum."

When astronomer Percival Lowell announced in 1906 that he had seen canals on Mars, the academic world was suitably impressed. Later, in his book *Mars as the Abode of Life*, Lowell wrote that the canals were red and seemed to move. His charts of the canals were included in atlases and schoolbooks.

The problem is that there are no canals on Mars. The eminent astronomer was suffering from a rare eye disease now called Lowell's syndrome. The canals he saw were actually the veins of his own eyes.

Silver has what chemists call a positive standard reduction potential, which means that it draws electrons from other metals. That's why it's so painful to chew on a piece of aluminum foil if you have silver fillings in your teeth. Your mildly acidic saliva acts as a catalyst and sets up a flow of electrons from foil to filling. A crude electric battery is created and the current flowing through the nerves of your teeth causes the distinctly unpleasant sensation.

Quiz· In which three sports is left-handed play illegal? (Answer: page 93)

❝ The most remarkable thing about my mother is that for 30 years she served the family nothing but leftovers. The original meal has never been found. ❞
~Calvin Trillin

The name "cesarean" for the operation to deliver a baby through an incision in the abdomen comes from the Latin verb *caedere*, to cut, and has nothing whatsoever to do with Julius Caesar.

In Spokane, Washington, a divorce was granted to a woman who said her husband criticized her cooking once too often. The final straw was when he used a hatchet to carve her Christmas turkey.

Gregor Mendel, the Bohemian monk whose experiments breeding peas founded the science of genetics and provided a basis for the theory of evolution, may have fudged his results. Scientists who have studied Mendel's original data say the numbers are just too good to be true. The monk, they say, made arithmetic errors almost always in his own favor, omitted data that didn't fit, and gave himself the benefit of every doubt. His observed ratios of dominant and submissive traits matched the theoretical predictions too closely, lacking the normal range of variabilities, so that the odds are overwhelming that such exactitude didn't arise by chance. The conclusion, in other words, is that Mendel cheated. ~Photo courtesy of Culver Pictures

MOVE OVER, NIELSEN

.{ The Waterworks Department of Lafayette, Louisiana, monitored the water pressure of the city one evening when the movie *Airport* was showing on TV. Their report: "At approximately 8:30, a bomb exploded in the airplane, and from then until nine p.m., when the pilot landed safely and the movie ended, almost nobody left his television set to do anything—then there was a twenty-six-pound drop in water pressure."

Twenty thousand viewers, it was estimated, all went to their bathrooms at the end of the movie and simultaneously flushed away thousands of gallons of city water. The water department figures turned out to be an excellent measure of the popularity of TV movies. By comparison, *The Good, the Bad, and the Ugly* was credited with producing a nineteen-pound drop in the city's water pressure, while *Patton*, starring George C. Scott, got a twenty-two-pound rating on the flush meter.

{ Bush pilots often fly low over herds of cattle to tell what the wind direction is at ground level. Cattle have sweat glands in their noses. They face into the wind on hot days to cool themselves and away from the wind in cold weather to keep warmer.

{ Vivien Leigh refused to continue playing love scenes with her costar in *Gone With the Wind* unless he did something about his bad breath. It seems that Clark Gable's dentures were so bad they produced a foul odor and Leigh found it difficult to act smitten anywhere near him.

CAT-APULT WAR

.{ King Cambyses I of Anshan, a region of ancient Persia, used cats to force the surrender of the Egyptian city of Memphis in the sixth century B.C. Cambyses knew that cats were sacred to Egyptians, so he ordered his soldiers to grab as many stray felines as they could find and sling them over the walls of Memphis. Appalled, the Egyptians quickly surrendered rather than witness further desecration.

{ Buy a large bucket of popcorn in the theater and you'll pay two to three dollars. It cost the owners about thirty-two cents, according to a recent report, so the retail markup is about 600 to 900 percent. The cost breakdown is as follows: five cents for the popcorn, two cents for the butter substitute, and twenty-five cents for the bucket.

The most common first name in the world is Mohammed. The most common last name in the world is Chan.

THE BULLET AND THE BABY

{ "During the fray [between Union and Confederate forces], a [soldier] staggered and fell to earth; at the same time a piercing cry was heard in the house near by. Examination of the wounded soldier showed that a bullet had passed through the scrotum and carried away the left testicle. The same bullet had apparently penetrated the left side of the abdomen of . . . [a] young lady midway between the umbilicus and the anterior spinous process of the ileum, and become lost in the abdomen. This daughter suffered an attack of peritonitis, but recovered . . . Two hundred and seventy-eight days after the reception of the minié ball, she was delivered of a fine boy, weighing eight pounds, to the surprise of herself and the mortification of her parents and friends . . . The doctor . . . concluded that . . . the same ball that had carried away the testicle of his young friend . . . had penetrated the ovary of the young lady, and, with some spermatazoa upon it, had impregnated her. With this conviction he approached the young man and told him the circumstances. The soldier appeared skeptical at first, but consented to visit the young mother; a friendship ensued which soon ripened into a happy marriage."

~ *The American Weekly*, November 4, 1874, quoted in Gould and Pyle, *Anomalies and Curiosities of Medicine*. Philadelphia: The Julien Press, 1896

Why do the fire engines in La Paz, Bolivia, go unused? Because the city is almost fireproof. At twelve thousand feet above sea level there is barely enough oxygen to support combustion.

The Twenty-third Psalm's "He leadeth me beside the still waters" refers to the fact that sheep refuse to drink from running water.

TINY TIMBER

{ The smallest trees in the world are dwarf willows. They grow only two inches high on the tundra of Greenland.

CHAIN MAIL

It is illegal to send chain letters in the U.S. mail. They are officially banned by fraud laws, but prosecutors find it hard to make the laws stick. Since chain letters all include the proviso, "If no one breaks the chain," there's technically nothing fraudulent about them. Inevitably someone will break the chain, and that can make a lot of people lose a lot of money, but if the wording of the letters is taken literally, there's no fraud there. It would be just as illogical to charge a stockbroker with fraud if he or she promises you big profits on investments "so long as current market trends continue."

Gary Cooper was right-handed. In The Pride of the Yankees he had to give a convincing portrayal of great lefty Lou Gehrig. In still photos like this and in some scenes of the movie, Cooper wore a glove on his right hand and threw and batted left-handed. For more active sequences some camera trickery was used. He wore a uniform with the letters sewn on in reverse, and was photographed on third instead of Gehrig's first-base position. Shots of the star throwing, fielding and batting were printed on the reverse side of the film, so that when the movie was screened normally, Cooper looked like a natural lefty. ~Photo courtesy of Culver Pictures

Quiz. Kay Thompson's book Eloise, *the story of a little girl who lived at the Plaza Hotel in New York, was inspired by the real adventures of Thompson's own goddaughter, who grew up in pampered surroundings and was destined for a life of fame. Who was she? (Answer: Page 93)*

Rum is sometimes known as "Nelson's blood" because Admiral Horatio Nelson's body was carried back to England in a cask of shipboard rum when he died. Sailors tapped the cask anyway, apparently not caring that the admiral's blood was part of their cocktails.

A one-pack-per-day cigarette smoker consumes four hundred milligrams of nicotine in a week. That would be enough to cause instant death if taken in one dose.

A cow spends eighteen hours of every day chewing.

SMOG ALERT

When Los Angeles County Supervisor Kenneth Hahn wrote to the Ford Motor Company about the air pollution in L.A., and expressed his concern that automobile exhausts contributed to the problem, he got a letter back from Dan J. Chabek, official spokesman for Ford company engineers, which concluded, "The Ford engineering staff, although mindful that automobile engines produce exhaust gases, feels these waste vapors are dissipated in the atmosphere quickly and do not present an air pollution problem."

That was Ford Motors' official position on the pollution problem, as of March 1953.

ABSENTEE HONOREE

Yale University is named for a man who never set foot in the United States after age three, when he moved to England with his parents. After Elihu Yale retired as governor of the East India Company, Cotton Mather, the ambassador of a fledgling Connecticut college, got Yale to donate some money, books, and a painting of George I, and in return got the school to change its name from Collegiate School of Connecticut to Yale in 1718. If Yale was appreciative he didn't show it. He died a wealthy man three years later but left nothing more in his will to the college overseas that had honored him and that still carries his name.

❧ In 1982, the Democratic vote in Texas was so strong that it swept a dead man into office. John Wilson was reelected to the state senate with 66 percent of the vote in his district, even though he had died of cancer during the campaign.

Quiz. Calvin Coolidge was once approached at a dinner party by a fatuous woman who said she was sure she could draw out the taciturn President in conversation. "My husband has bet me that I won't be able to get more than three words out of you," she gushed. What was Silent Cal's classic reply? (Answer: page 93)

❧ When providing testimony as an expert witness, Henry Augustus Rowland (1848–1901) was asked to name the greatest physicist in America.

"I myself am," Rowland replied.

Since Rowland was known to be an extremely modest man, a friend asked him after the trial why he had given such an unusually egotistical answer.

"I couldn't help it, I was under oath," Rowland said.

INTERCEPTING A PASS

❧ Homosexual British biographer Lytton Strachey was compelled to appear before a military draft tribunal to defend his conscientious objection to army service during World War I. One of the examiners, trying to show that Strachey's pacifism wasn't genuine, asked him what he would do if he saw a German soldier trying to rape his sister. "I would try to get between them," was Strachey's reply.

❧ An Australian housewife named Maud Walker was so overcome with excitement after winning big on the TV game show "Temptation" that she suffered a fatal on-camera heart attack. A station executive tried to soothe the Walker family's grief by offering them a video recording of the show. "I'm sure they would like to see how happy she was," he said.

Nancy Reagan's friend Betsy Bloomingdale said that one of the ways she saved energy was "by asking my servants not to turn on the self-cleaning oven until after seven in the morning."

What cemetery is most famous for its celebrities? Père-Lachaise cemetery in Paris is the last resting place of some of the world's biggest names: Chopin, Balzac, Daumier, Wilde, Molière, Rossini, Bizet, Sarah Bernhardt—and Rin Tin Tin. The original Rin Tin Tin was found as a puppy wandering between trenches in France in World War I. After a life as a Hollywood star, Rinty was returned to his native country for burial.

HER PARTS WERE RIGHT FOR THE PART

On the television series "Richard Diamond, Private Detective" the answering service girl, Sam, was shown only from the waist down. Her voice was heard, but the actress who played Sam got no screen credit for the role, and she played the part only from July 1957 to May 1959. It was her first part in a TV series, but there would be others that featured more than just the legs of Mary Tyler Moore.

Today the temperature in Quito, Ecuador, is probably 69, 70, or 71 degrees Fahrenheit. How do we know? Because temperatures in Quito are almost always in that narrow range. High-altitude locations near the equator have much the same weather year-round and the 9,300-foot-high capital of Ecuador, which is almost exactly on the earth's midline, is just such a place.

It's only the female mosquito that bites, and a well-fed lady skeeter can fly carrying twice her normal weight in blood. Male mosquitoes never bite anyone or anything; they feed entirely on plant juices.

Edward Hyde, the colonial governor of New York and New Jersey from 1702 to 1708, was an unashamed transvestite. He often paraded in public wearing a dress, makeup, and a woman's wig. His official portrait shows the governor resplendent in a low-cut evening gown and holding a fan. He was relieved of his duties in 1708, but his confused sexual identity had nothing to do with it—he was found guilty of taking bribes.

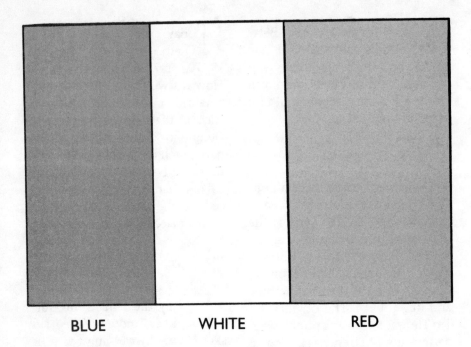

BLUE   WHITE   RED

LIBERTÉ, FRATERNITÉ, INÉGALITÉ

Human perception is tricky and often produces distortions, but sometimes artists purposely use distortions to make things look more real. The flag of France has three vertical stripes—blue, white, and red. If the three stripes were exactly the same width, the differing wavelengths of the colors would make the stripes appear different: the red band would seem to be narrower than the others, for example. To counteract this, the French flag is designed so the three bands will appear to be equal. Actually, they are in a proportion of 100 for the blue, 110 for the white, and 124 for the red.

Greek architects knew about perception tricks like this when they built the Parthenon and made the columns widen slightly at the top. If the columns were perfectly perpendicular, they would appear to lean inward at the top, as seen by an observer on the ground. To counteract this, columns of the Parthenon (and similar structures such as the Lincoln Memorial in Washington, D.C.) actually lean outward slightly at the top so that they will appear straight to the eye.

British author John Galsworthy was desperate for a quiet place to finish his play *Justice*, so he threw a brick through a storefront window and finished the play during a six-month jail sentence.

POLISH ECONOMICS: CREDIT WHERE IT'S DUE

If you buy something that costs a dollar and you have two one-dollar bills in your wallet or purse, one a crisp, clean, newly minted dollar and the other a wrinkled, faded dollar, chances are you'll give the clerk the old bill and keep the new one. In economics this principle, which explains why old currency remains in circulation while new currency tends to be hoarded (summarized as, "Bad money drives out good"), is known in dictionaries as "Gresham's Law," after Sir Thomas Gresham, the English financier who supposedly first formulated the idea.

But according to Isaac Asimov, the true originator of the law was none other than Nicolaus Copernicus, the Polish astronomer best remembered for insisting that the earth revolves around the sun, and not vice versa. Copernicus was a man of many talents and he first coined the idea, decades before Gresham did, that money of lesser intrinsic value drives good money into hiding as part of his work in currency reform.

Which raft will float fastest down a river—a heavily loaded one or an empty one? Surprisingly, the full raft will move faster because it lies deeper in the water.

BOOKLEARNING

"The mental constitution of the negro is . . . normally good-natured and cheerful, but subject to sudden fits of emotion and passion during which he is capable of performing acts of singular atrocity, impressionable, vain, but often exhibiting in the capacity of servant a dog-like fidelity which has stood the supreme test. . . . [After puberty, however] sexual matters take first place in the negro's life and thoughts."

This passage was not penned by a modern white supremacist. Walter Francis Willcox, Chief Statistician for the U.S. Census Bureau, wrote it in his entry under "Negro" for the 1911 edition of the *Encyclopaedia Britannica*.

What do Noel Coward, Thomas Edison, Sean O'Casey, Charles Dickens, and Mark Twain have in common? None ever completed grade school.

Charles Lindbergh experimented with the preservation of human organs removed from the body and published a book on the subject, *The Culture of Organs*, with French scientist Alexis Carrel. Lindbergh's investigations led him to perfect one of the first mechanical hearts to pump blood to organs outside the body.

THE WIDE WORLD OF SPORTS

In the 1900 Olympics in Paris, there was competition in checkers, billiards, and fishing (in the Seine)—but since these were demonstration sports, no medals were awarded. Since the contests weren't picked up in subsequent games the world was spared an Olympic gold medalist in checkers.

Abdul Kassem Ismael, the grand-vizier of Persia from 938 to 995 A.D., took his entire collection of 117,000 books with him on his travels. The vizier's camel-driver librarians could quickly locate any volume their master asked for, because the animals were trained to walk in alphabetical order.

It's comforting to know that the purple dye our government uses to stamp approval on meat is made from edible material—grape skins, in fact.

Squirrels can climb trees faster than they can run on the ground.

The first child to be vaccinated against smallpox in Russia was named Vaccinov and educated at national expense. It was a gesture of thanks for Edward Jenner's discovery of the smallpox vaccine.

Quiz Answers

Page 78: The strawberry.

Page 79: The pear grew inside the bottle. In orchards where this is done, mostly in France, Italy, and Spain, bottles are placed over pear buds when they are small and are wired in place on the tree, as shown above. The bottle is left in place for the whole growing season, which may be four months or more. When the pears are ripe, workers snip them off at the stems. The bottles are then cleaned inside and out, the brandy is added, and the bottles are sealed and shipped off to market.

It's a lot of work to create a conversation piece, but many brandy buyers are willing to pay for the novelty.

Page 81: Piecrust.

Page 83: Jai alai, polo, and field hockey. Left-handed play is illegal in these sports because it is considered too dangerous. Field hockey sticks are asymmetrical and only the left, flat side of the blade may be used to strike the ball.

Page 87: Liza Minnelli

Page 88: "You lose."

THE LEANING TOWER OF NILES

Robert A Ilg, a millionaire businessman, built this unusual home—a half-scale replica of the Leaning Tower of Pisa—right in the heart of Niles, Illinois, a suburb of Chicago, in 1932. He constructed everything on a permanent eleven-degree slant. Ilg lived in his leaning tower for seventeen summers, then finally moved to California to reside in an ordinary level house. ~Photo by Bob Riemer, courtesy of Chicago Historical Society

THE BOOK THAT GOT INTO ITSELF

The *Guinness Book of World Records* was first published in 1955. Nineteen years later, in 1974, it got into itself: it had set a record as the fastest-selling book in the world.

A "fiasco" is a complete failure. The word comes from the glass blower's art in ancient Venice. If a fine glass crystal was ruined by mistake the only way the glass blower could salvage it was to turn it into a *fiasco*, the Italian word for an ordinary drinking flask.

Victoe Biaka-Boda, a representative of the Ivory Coast in the French senate, went on a tour of his homeland in order to meet the people he was representing and get to know their problems. Undernourishment was a problem he didn't anticipate solving quite as he did. In January 1950, Biaka-Boda was captured and eaten by his constituents.

Thomas Edison proposed to his wife in Morse code. Edison suffered from deafness and he taught his future wife the dot-and-dash code while he was courting her. Edison popped the question by squeezing out the message while they held hands. Her reply, again conveyed by hand, was $-\cdot--, \cdot, \cdots$.

In every U.S. presidential election since the turn of the century, the taller of the two candidates won.

When a Christian fundamentalist group in Columbus, Ohio, wanted to ban E. B. White's classic children's book *Charlotte's Web* from school libraries, they based their objections on the character of Wilbur, a farm girl's pet pig who has conversations with other farm animals. At a fund-raiser, passages of pig talk were read aloud and denounced as ungodly. Wilbur, they said, was a blasphemous creation. The reason? It is against God's will for animals to talk.

THE SHOW GOES ON

Actor Orson Welles broke his ankle in January 1956, but didn't let that stop him from his engagement at New York's City Center. In the performance of *King Lear*, Welles played the title role entirely from a wheelchair.

Jersey Joe Walcott's real name was Arnold Cream.

HOW TO TRICK A POINSETTIA

Many people throw their Christmas poinsettias away after the holiday season because, although the plants will grow indoors all year if properly cared for, they will not turn red the following December. That's because the plant comes into flower only in response to the shorter days of autumn. You can fool a poinsettia, however. After the color disappears in spring, cut the plant back to about six inches and let it grow over the summer. In October or November, stimulate the flowering by covering the plant with a plastic garbage bag at 5 P.M. and removing it at 8 A.M. The plant's chemistry will tell it that the seasons are changing and winter is coming, and the leaves will soon begin to turn red.

In 1913, Lee de Forest was trying to sell stock in his Radio Telephone Company and he told potential investors that in the near future it would be possible to transmit the human voice across the Atlantic on radio waves. He was prosecuted for fraud and brought to trial. The district attorney accused him of making "absurd and deliberately misleading statements." De Forest and radio won.

Quiz. *Milk keeps longest in what kind of container—the glass bottle, the plastic bottle, or the paper carton? (Answer: page 107)*

The windiest city in the United States is Fargo, North Dakota, where winds average 14.4 m.p.h. By contrast, the winds in Chicago, the Windy City, average only 10.6 m.p.h. Actually, Chicago didn't get its nickname from the way the breezes blow there. Charles Dana, a writer for the New York Sun, coined the name in 1893 as a slap at Chicagoans for all the bragging they were doing about the World's Fair being held in their city that year.

DOCTOR'S ORDERS

How do you spell relief from arthritis pain? S-E-X. That's the conclusion of Dr. Jessie Potter of the University of Illinois and Northwestern University medical schools. Potter told a meeting of the National Arthritis Foundation that sexual activity stimulates the adrenal glands to release cortisone, which can give arthritis patients four to six hours of pain relief.

STRANGEST STEAL

Germany Schaefer, a player with the Washington Senators, once did something on the field that changed the rules of baseball. He stole second base with a man on third, hoping the catcher would try to throw him out so that his teammate could attempt to steal home. The catcher didn't throw to second, so on the next pitch Schaefer *stole first* to try again. When the confusion died down the strange steal was deemed to be legal—just that once. A new rule (number 7.08(i)) was immediately added to the game, making it illegal for a player to run the bases in reverse.

Carefully recorded in Kentucky Marriages 1797–1865 is the wedding on June 11, 1831, of Moses Alexander, age 93, to his blushing bride Frances Tompkins, 105. A following entry reports that Mr. and Mrs. Alexander were both found dead in their bed the next morning.

❝ You just sat there thinking that this piece of hardware had 400,000 components, all of them built by the lowest bidder. **❞**

~David Scott, Apollo 15 astronaut, on the blast-off

LONG PONG

{ After the opening serve in a Swaythling Cup match in table tennis, in Prague on March 14, 1936, Alex Ehrlich of Poland and his opponent, Paneth Farcas of Rumania, rallied for one hour and fifty-eight minutes before the first point was scored.

{ Why is Christ's face almost indistinguishable in Da Vinci's *Last Supper*? During the Napoleonic Wars, French soldiers who were camped in Milan near the chapel of *Santa Maria delle Grazie* used the painting on the wall of the church for target practice.

SPRING CLEANING

{ Every citizen of Kentucky was once required by law to take a bath at least once a year. Last we heard, the law was still on the books—not many legislators have wanted to repeal it.

❝The only job in the whole world I want to do is acting. Offer me ten times the money for doing something else and I'd refuse. I'd lack self-confidence because I'd be in the wrong job.**❞**
~Ronald Reagan, 1942

Hetty Green, "the witch of Wall Street," had built a $6 million inheritance, through a long series of brilliant stock market coups, into a fortune estimated at over $100 million. By the time of her death, in 1916, she was said to be the richest woman in the world. But she lived the life of a miserly pauper.

Hetty Green wore the same dress every day. She used newspapers pulled from trash cans as undergarments and refused to heat her tenement home or even to cook her meals (she ate mostly dry oatmeal) to save on her fuel bill. When her son Edward, aged nine, was run over by a wagon and injured a leg, Hetty refused to call a doctor (who would charge her money) and instead took the boy to a number of free clinics. Eventually the boy's leg had to be amputated. ~Photo courtesy of Culver Pictures

A man's body is about 70 percent water. A woman's body is only 60 percent water. The difference explains why a woman gets drunk faster than a man after consuming an equal amount of alcohol, even when both weigh the same. The extra water dilutes the man's alcohol slightly.

Quiz· *Only three words in standard English begin with the letters* dw. *They are all common. Can you name two of them? (Answer: page 107)*

UNTIMELY MISTAKE

The March 21, 1983, issue of Time magazine featured Lee Iacocca on the cover along with a teaser for Henry Kissinger's "New Plan for Arms Control."

After two hundred thousand of the covers had been printed, someone noticed a typographical error —the r had been left out of "Control." It was printed as *Contol*.

There had never been a misspelling on a Time cover in the history of the magazine. The editors had but one choice. They stopped the presses, corrected the error, and withdrew all the "Contol" covers. The goof cost Time $100,000, and 40 percent of its newsstand copies went on sale a day late.

RELATIVELY WRONG

66 *There is not the slightest indication that [nuclear] energy will ever be obtainable. It would mean that the atom would have to be shattered at will.* 99
~Albert Einstein, 1932

The California town of Tarzana was named for Tarzan, the hero of the jungle books and movies created by Edgar Rice Burroughs, who was the town's most famous resident for many years. The town of Modesto, California, was named to honor its founders— they were too "modest" to name it after themselves.

No one ever accused John Ringling North of thinking small when promoting The Greatest Show on Earth. He once staged an "elephant ballet," with original music written by Igor Stravinsky and with the pachyderm's steps choreographed by George Balanchine.

An alligator can snap its jaws shut with bone-breaking power. But the muscles to open an alligator's jaws are so weak that a man can easily hold them shut with one hand. ~Photo by Julian Dimock, courtesy of Department of Library Services, American Museum of Natural History

Rain is good for wicker lawn furniture. Wicker lasts longer if it gets wet now and then.

Boulder Dam's base is 660 feet thick, about the length of a city block.

When Dorothy Parker arrived at a Halloween party hosted by Herbert Bayard Swope, she noticed the other guests playing a game and asked what it was.

"They're ducking for apples," Swope said.

"There, but for a typographical error," Parker sighed, "is the story of my life."

Quiz· There are fourteen punctuation marks in English grammar. Can you name more than half of them? (Answer: page 107)

❝I hate to advocate drugs, alcohol, violence or insanity to anyone, but they've always worked for me.❞
~Hunter S. Thompson

Charles Dickens always wrote facing north, and slept with his head to the north, in order to align himself with the earth's poles.

Quiz. Residents on the Danish island of Mano have cars and regularly drive them to Jutland, on the mainland. There are no bridges or tunnels between the island and mainland Denmark, however. How do the Manoans commute? (Answer: page 107)

ROYALTIES EVEN FOR RERUNS

Every time Doc Severinsen leads the band to introduce Johnny Carson, Paul Anka gets another two hundred dollars. The fee is a royalty for "The Tonight Show" theme music, which Anka composed in collaboration with Carson in 1962.

Confederate general Thomas "Stonewall" Jackson died after being shot accidentally by his own troops at the battle of Chancellorsville in 1863.

WOULD THE UTOPIAN TURTLETOP HAVE SOLD BETTER?

In the late 1950s, when the Ford Motor Company was searching for a name for a new medium-priced car it was developing, David Wallace, director of planning for Market Research, got advice from the wife of a junior executive at Ford. The young woman had recently graduated from Mount Holyoke College, where she had heard the poet Marianne Moore and was impressed with her way with words. The woman suggested that Wallace ask Miss Moore what she would call the car, and Wallace liked the idea. "We should like this name," he wrote to the famous poet, ". . . to convey, through association or other conjuration, some visceral feeling of elegance, fleetness, advanced features and design."

Moore suggested such names as the Intelligent Bullet, Andante con Moto, Pastelogram, Bullet Cloisonné, and Utopian Turtletop. Ford executives passed by all these names and chose to call the car, instead, the Edsel.

❝ I think it would be a good idea. ❞
~Mahatma Gandhi, asked what he
thought of Western civilization

WASN'T THE FUTURE WONDERFUL?

At the 1939–40 New York World's Fair the General Motors "futurama" exhibit included these predictions of what life would be like in America in the 1960s: "People do not care much for possessions. Two-month paid vacations. Cars are air-conditioned and cost as little as $200. The happiest people live in one-factory villages."

The Mona Lisa has no eyebrows. Renaissance fashion in Florence called for ladies to shave them off.

Charles Goodyear started the experiments that led to vulcanized rubber when he was in prison. Jailed for debts in 1834, he started tests with rubber while in his cell.

HE KNEW THE SCORE, BUT NOT THE GAME

It wasn't until twenty years after he wrote "Take Me Out to the Ball Game" that Albert von Tilzer actually saw his first one.

On November 12, 1955, an intercollegiate football game was played between San Jose State and Washington State. The weather was brutal in Pullman, Washington, that day, with a zero-degree temperature and chilling winds that whipped through the stadium. The total paid attendance at the game was one.

Actress Sarah Bernhardt played the role of Juliet, in Shakespeare's play Romeo and Juliet, when she was seventy years old.

The flying of flags at half-mast is a universal indication of mourning. As the term "half-mast" suggests, the custom has a nautical origin. In the days of sailing ships, military vessels indicated a death aboard, or the death of a national leader, by slacking their rigging, trailing the lines, and allowing the yardarms to tilt so that the ship presented a purposely disheveled appearance, symbolizing sorrow. The half-masting of colors is a holdover from the days when a ship's slovenly look was the nautical equivalent of walking around in sackcloth and ashes.

“Die? Die, my dear doctor? That's the last thing I shall do!”

~Viscount Palmerston, on his deathbed, 1865

RIPE BUT NOT READY

Squash and pumpkin seeds become more nutritious as they decompose. After five months of storage, the seeds actually showed an increase in protein content in tests made at the Massachusetts Experimental Station.

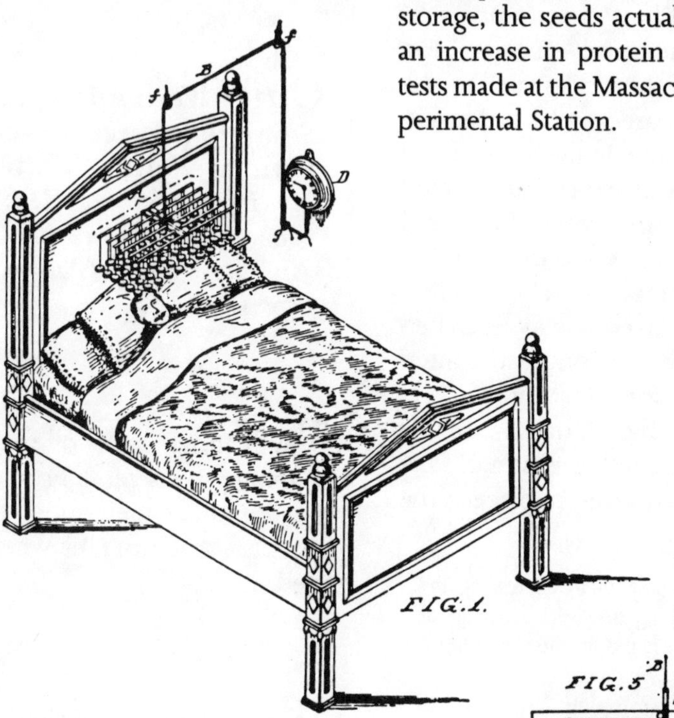

FIG. 1.

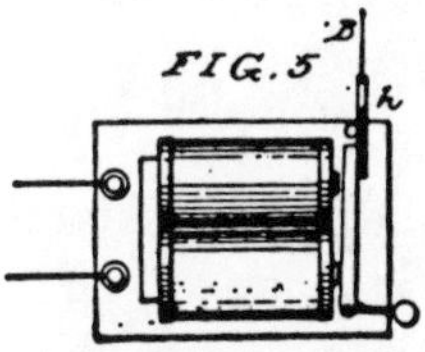

FIG. 5

THE ULTIMATE ALARM CLOCK

Alarm clocks sometimes don't serve their purpose, because in time the user becomes accustomed to the bell or buzzer and is no longer awakened by it. Here's a solution designed to do away with that problem forever. In this patent by Samuel S. Applegate of Camden, New Jersey (No. 256,265, issued in 1882), the whole bed becomes the alarm clock. Above the bed is a frame from which pieces of cork or wood hang by many cords. At the wake-up hour "the frame is . . . permitted to fall into the sleeper's face." That should wake even those who sleep through chimes and bells, Applegate reasoned, "the only necessity to be observed in constructing the frame being that when it falls it will strike a light blow, sufficient to awaken the sleeper, but not heavy enough to cause pain." ~Reproduced with permission from *Mousetraps and Muffling Cups* by Kenneth Lasson

REJECTION SLIP

{ "Before *The World According to Garp* was published," author John Irving wrote, "I decided to submit the best short story contained in the novel—'The Pension Grillparzer,' the work which begins T. S. Garp's career—to a serious literary magazine. In the novel, I had written that the story was rejected by such a magazine; I guess I wanted to see what would really happen to this story. The rejection I, in fact, received was so much better than the rejection I had written (fictionally) for the story that I revised the final draft of the book by including the *real* rejection of 'The Pension Grillparzer' in place of the one I'd made up . . .

> The story is only mildly interesting, and it does nothing new with language or with form. Thanks for showing it to us, though.
> —The Paris Review

"My editor later asked if I didn't think I was going too far. That was when I showed him the original. Of course the editor then agreed to let the rejection stand.

"I tried the story with *American Review*, too; they turned it down. And even two non-literary magazines didn't want it: *The New Yorker* and *Esquire*. It was a good feeling when 'The Pension Grillparzer' was repeatedly singled out as one of the strongest parts of the novel, and it won the Pulitzer Prize for short fiction that year. One literary magazine, *Antaeus*, did publish it. Naturally, I've liked them ever since."

Quiz. When a 165-year-old white oak tree was cut down at Rutgers University in September 1963, it caused a furor among students. Why? (Answer: page 107)

The natural color of the flamingo is not pink. Flamingos are colored by their food, blue-green algae that turn pink when digested.

{ Why do men like to sing in the shower more than women apparently do? Bathroom tile resonates to bass and baritone notes, but not to the higher soprano. Men's voices sound better in the bathroom.

{ The inventor of dynamite, Alfred Nobel, was also the inventor of plywood and one of the first designers of prefabricated housing.

Quiz. There are 1064 seashells here, arranged by Ken Knowlton (see page 2, domino portrait of Groucho Marx). The work is four feet tall and is displayed on a wall at San Francisco's science museum, the Exploratorium. Stand close to the work and you see just shells, bits of coral and ocean debris, all gathered from one beach in Puerto Rico. Viewers must walk several yards away from the work before they see a face in the rectangle. It's a specific face. Can you tell who it is? (Answer: page 107).   ~Photo by Ken Knowlton

William Beebe built a submersible enclosure for exploring the ocean bottom, to be suspended by cables from a boat on the surface. His original plan was to make the vessel in the shape of a cylinder. A friend suggested that a spherical shape would be stronger. Beebe took his advice, and the bathysphere was born. The friend's name was Franklin D. Roosevelt. ~Photo courtesy of New York Zoological Society

Quiz Answers

Page 97: Paper cartons work best, it has been found, because paper blocks most of the fluorescent light used in many store displays and home kitchens, which can cause milk to deteriorate.

Page 99: Dwarf, dwell, and dwindle.

Page 100: Period, comma, colon, semicolon, dash, hyphen, apostrophe, question mark, exclamation point, quotation marks, brackets, parentheses, braces, and ellipses.

Page 101: They drive on the bottom of the sea. There's a road on the seabed, lined with trees, that is only open for a few hours a day, at low tide. At high tide the road is covered by five feet of water.

Page 104: It was said to be the tree that had inspired Joyce Kilmer to write his famous poem "Trees."

Page 105: The face in the seashells is, appropriately, Jacques Cousteau.

*S*itting Bull, shown here, didn't always sit: he started life as Jumping Badger. It was the custom among some American Indian tribes to give newborn boys temporary names. The names were changed later, as the boys developed character and showed courage in manhood. One Sioux boy, first called Curly, later in life got the more memorable name Crazy Horse. ~Photo courtesy of National Archives

CHAPTER

8

SNIPING SEXOLOGIST

Sex therapist Dr. Ruth West-heimer once lived in Israel, where she was a trained sniper. She was so adept at handling a Sten gun—a British submachine gun—that she could put one together while blindfolded.

The driest place in the world is the Atacama desert along the Pacific in Chile. In some places there no rainfall has ever been recorded.

In 1978 there was a reported 60 percent drop in human organs donated to U.S. hospitals, as com-pared to the previous year. Why? Kidney-transplant surgeon James Cerilli theorized it was a national scare stirred up by a movie. The decline in donors occurred just after the release of *Coma*, a 1978 film in which hospital patients are murdered so their organs can be harvested and sold.

UNDERSTANDABLE SUPERSTITION

In many hospitals in Japan there are no rooms numbered four or nine. Why? In the Japanese lan-guage, the word for "four" sounds the same as the word for "death," and the word for "nine" is a hom-onym of the word for "suffering."

Horses can sleep standing up.

Mystery writer Dashiell Hammett was once a detective with the Pinkerton agency. He got his first promotion for bringing in a man who had stolen a Ferris wheel.

The National Coalition on Television Violence ranked TV shows according to the number of violent acts shown per hour. "Miami Vice" logged in with an average of 31 acts of violence per hour, but the show that topped the list, with 301 violent acts an hour, was a rerun of a 1950s World War II documentary series, *Victory at Sea*.

Dr. Kissinger's real name is Heinz, not Henry.

Quiz· *Because of its kaolin mines (kaolin is a porous type of clay), the city of Quincy, Florida, is nicknamed "The [something] capital of the world." What's the something? (Answer: page 121)*

BEAUTY IN THE VOID

❝ One of the most beautiful sights is a urine dump at sunset, because as the stuff comes out [in space] and as it hits the exit nozzle, it instantly flashes into 10 million little ice crystals, which go out almost in a hemisphere, because, you know, you're exiting into essentially a perfect vacuum, and so the stuff goes in every direction, and radially out from the spacecraft at relatively high velocity. It's surprising, and it's an incredible . . . spray of sparklers almost. It's really a spectacular sight. **❞**

~Russell Schweickart, Apollo astronaut

The state of Wisconsin is divided into voting wards for elections. One ward of five hundred residents is in Adams County, but none of the residents can cast a ballot. They're in a federal correctional institution, which makes up the entire ward.

HE DID CREATE THE CODE, HOWEVER

Samuel F. B. Morse did not invent the telegraph, as he claimed to. Morse got all necessary information for the invention from American physicist Joseph Henry, then denied Henry had helped him. Henry promptly took Morse to court, and won.

Quiz. Where are the lakes that are referred to in "Lakers," the name of the Los Angeles basketball team? (Answer: page 121)

In St. John, New Brunswick, there is a waterfall that at times becomes a "water rise." It is on a river gorge leading into the Bay of Fundy. Tidal variations there are enormous, and during high tide the water level in the bay can be five feet higher than in its tributary river. A tidal bore then flows upriver, resulting in the Reversing Falls of St. John.

The annual output of a single coffee tree amounts to about one pound of ground coffee.

Rubies, sapphires, aquamarines, and emeralds are two minerals—not four. Corundum comes in a red variety (called the ruby) and a blue variety (the sapphire). Similarly, aquamarines and emeralds are both beryls—the blue kind and the green kind, respectively.

It was an insult, of course, but it also made an excellent alibi. When a women's collective claimed responsibility for bombing Harvard's Center for International Affairs in October 1970, the Cambridge police didn't believe them. "This was a sophisticated bomb," said a police spokesman. "We feel that women wouldn't be capable of making such a bomb."

Police uniforms were introduced for the first time in New York City in 1844. The peace officers at first refused to come to work wearing matching outfits, saying that dressing in uniforms was fit only for maids and butlers.

Ninety-nine percent of all forms of life that have existed on earth are now extinct.

The last words Abraham Lincoln ever heard were "You sockdologizing old mantrap!" The audience roared with laughter at this line in the play *Our American Cousin*, spoken by actor Asa Trenchard. John Wilkes Booth timed his assassination and used the laughter at this line to cover the sound of his gunshots.

SPIES ON THE PUZZLE PAGE?

•{ When plans for the D-Day invasion were well under way, the British counterespionage service was shocked to find the words OVERLORD, NEPTUNE, UTAH, OMAHA, and MULBERRY in a *Daily Telegraph* crossword puzzle. They were afraid the top-secret operation had been compromised.

OVERLORD was the code word for the Normandy landing, UTAH and OMAHA were names given to beaches where American forces would land, MULBERRY designated a floating port the Allies planned to build once the beaches were secure, and NEPTUNE was a code word for D-Day naval support.

British intelligence subjected one Leonard Dawe, a schoolteacher in Surrey who compiled the newspaper crossword, to an intensive grilling before concluding that Dawe was not a German spy. The incident turned out to be a total coincidence.

{ In the decade 1963–73 some 46,752 Americans were killed in Vietnam. During that period almost twice as many Americans —84,633—died from gunshot wounds in the United States.

{ William Shakespeare earned his income not as a playwright but as a part owner of the Lord Chamberlain's Men, proprietors of the Globe Playhouse, where many of his works were staged. The Bard often acted in his own plays—playing the Ghost in *Hamlet* and Adam in *As You Like It.*

•{ Water draining from Mount Fuji in Japan is very polluted. You could take snapshots of the mountain, then develop your film in the highly alkaline water.

{ Hawaii and Arizona are the only states that have not adopted Daylight Savings Time.

{ When Lisbon, Portugal, was devastated by an earthquake and a tidal wave in 1755, some ministers in Boston had an unusual explanation: it was Benjamin Franklin's invention of the lightning rod, three years earlier, that had caused an unleashing of God's wrath. The Lord was displeased at this sacrilegious human attempt to interfere with nature, they said, and was delivering this disaster as a punishment to all mankind.

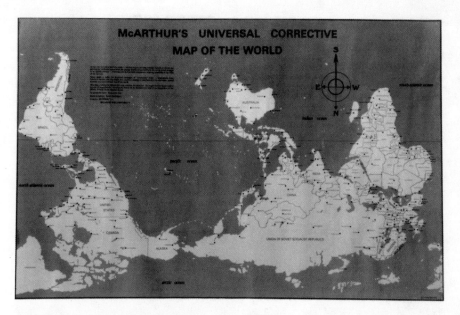

A WORLD TURNED UPSIDE DOWN

This map isn't printed upside down. It's the way it's supposed to be. Published in Australia, this is McArthur's Universal Corrective Map of the World. It shows what the world might look like if mapmaking had gotten its start in Australia rather than in southern Europe. The decision to print maps with "north up" is only a convention. The Earth is a spinning sphere in space, with no "top" or "bottom" side. One could just as easily view the planet from the other side, with the South Pole "up."

Two things stand out about this map. First, it is more pleasing aesthetically. Considering the land masses as abstract shapes, it is more natural to arrange them so the "weight" of the design is at the bottom. Second, the entire Pacific Ocean dominates the center, while the Atlantic Ocean is split up the middle and relegated to the two sides. In most traditional world maps the Atlantic Ocean is at the center: it was considered the "most important" ocean, flanked by the "most important" lands—the U.S.A. and Europe. The world has changed and the new upside-down map may show a more politically and economically relevant picture of today's planet, in which the powers around the Pacific rim are becoming more and more important, while the Atlantic is becoming the relatively "less important" ocean.   ∼Map courtesy of Rex Map Centres

:}{ Stevie Wonder endorses all contracts with his fingerprint.

NOT COUNTING OIL FOR THE LANTERNS

Paul Revere's patriotism didn't come cheap. To cover his expenses for that famous midnight ride he submitted an invoice to the state of Massachusetts for ten pounds, four shillings. The bill was paid.

LITERATURE AND LARD

Upton Sinclair published his novel The Jungle in 1906 to "frighten the country by a picture of what its masters were doing to their victims." While working in the Chicago stockyards, Sinclair had observed that poisoned bread and dead rats were swept onto a meat-conveyer belt and came out in sausages, and men who fell into open vats wound up in Anderson's Pure Beef Lard.

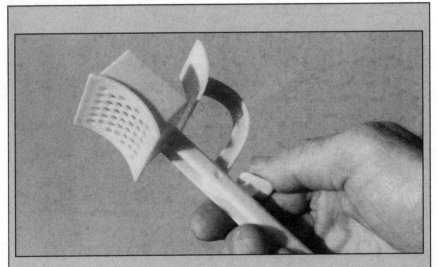

Whatzit Quiz

This tool is shaped like a garlic press: a square chamber with holes through its curved bottom is at one end, and a thumb piece pivots into the square chamber. But the bright yellow plastic is much too flimsy for pressing garlic. The tool is intended to be used at a dining room table. What is it? (Answer: page 121) ~Photo by Scot Morris

❝ My reaction to porno films is as follows: After the first ten minutes, I want to go home and screw. After the first twenty minutes, I never want to screw again as long as I live. **❞**

~Erica Jong

The first fatal airplane accident in history occurred on September 17, 1908 when an airplane's propeller broke and sent the craft plunging a hundred and fifty feet to earth. The plane's sole passenger, Lieutenant Thomas E. Selfridge of the U.S. Signal Corps, was killed in the crash and the pilot suffered multiple hip and leg fractures. The pilot's name was Orville Wright.

Darwin's *Origin of Species* (1859) sold out its entire first edition in one day.

"Doctor Livingstone, I presume?" Before Henry Morton Stanley delivered that famous line, he fought in the U.S. Civil War—on both sides. In 1859, he moved from Great Britain to New Orleans. In 1861, at age twenty, he enlisted in the Confederate army, but was captured and imprisoned. In exchange for his release, Stanley then agreed to join the Union artillery.

BUT WHERE DO YOU CARRY THE PERMIT?

Luigi Barzini, a member of the Italian Parliament, proposed that a committee of beauty experts be formed to issue nudity permits only to good-looking applicants. Ugly people would be forbidden to appear naked in public.

French composer Charles-Henri Alkan was more interested in Jewish scholarship than in his music. One of the top pianists of his day, Alkan performed rarely, preferring to spend his time with his religious books. One day in 1888 a huge volume of the Torah fell from a shelf, fractured his skull, and killed him.

CLEANED-UP MAPS

Near Ontario, Oregon, is a field where prostitutes used to set up tents in which to service lonely shepherds. The area was called Whorehouse Meadow, but the U.S. Board on Geographic Names balked at printing that on maps. Despite objections of the locals, the government changed the name of the site to Naughty Girl Meadow. Censors also sanitized an Arizona mountain known as Nellie's Nipple by listing it on maps with the innocuous name College Peak.

Quiz. *Gabriel D. Fahrenheit devised a temperature scale by defining two fixed points. He assigned zero to the coldest temperature he could get in a brine mixture of saltwater and ice. What did he use to set the other fixed point on his scale? (Answer: page 121)*

PROPRIETARY POCKETS

{The distinctive stitch pattern on the back pockets of Levi's jeans is trademarked. The stitching was originally functional—it kept the cotton lining of the back pockets from buckling. When the company dropped the lining it kept the stitching, and got a trademark on the pattern in 1942. During World War II the company stopped sewing the curved flourishes on its jeans—it didn't look good to waste valuable thread for a mere "look" while the country was in a materials shortage. For the duration of the war the pattern wasn't sewn but was painted onto the back pockets of every pair of Levi's.

A male spider's penis is at the end of one leg.

In order to emphasize her lean, high-cheekboned beauty, Marlene Dietrich had all her upper molars removed.

Garo Yepremian was hired as a place-kicker for the Miami Dolphins in October 1966. A scant three weeks before his debut in the NFL, he had never seen a football game. Four months prior to that, he had never even seen a football.

Yepremian was born in Cyprus and lived most of his life in London, where he developed into a strong, accurate soccer kicker. While on a visit to a brother in Indianapolis in June 1966, he first learned about the American game of football. He decided to try his foot at it and was signed by the Dolphins four months later. ~Photo courtesy of UPI/Bettmann Newsphotos

·{After he was 90 there was only one food that John D. Rockefeller could tolerate, due to a deteriorating digestive system—human breast milk. A number of lactating women were put on the Rockefeller payroll to provide the millionaire's meals.

"If we have to start over again with another Adam and Eve, then I want them to be Americans and not Russians, and I want them to be on this continent and not in Europe."
~Senator Richard B. Russell, 1970, in voting his approval of an antiballistic missile

{Dylan Thomas' play Under Milk Wood is set in the fictional Welsh town of Llareggub. He came up with the name by spelling "bugger all" backward.

IT'S GOT A GOOD BEAT, AND YOU CAN SLEEP TO IT

{Doctors have found that a recording of a woman's heartbeat can have a calming effect on infants under two months of age: they cry less when the tape is played. Apparently the sounds remind the baby of the monotonous lub-dub, lub-dub it heard in its mother's womb. Some orchestral music has the same effect, according to one report. Dr. A. M. Grossman, in the Medical Tribune, wrote that Brahms' First Symphony "closely resembles the pulsations found in the intrauterine environment of the foetus."

·{Beautiful breasts have served as molds for drinking cups. Marc Antony drank from a goblet shaped around one of Cleopatra's breasts, and a cup molded on the breast of Marie Antoinette is on display at the porcelain factory in Sèvres, France.

NATURE'S FIRECRACKER

{Forest fires may be devastating, but they also start a remarkable natural process that leads to forest renewal. Pinecones explode when they get very hot—as anyone who ever threw one into a campfire knows. This sudden opening seems to be a built-in adaptation designed, in case of fire, to quickly release the seeds for the next generation of pines.

MAKING A CLEAN BREAK

Carolyn Matsumoto, twenty-five, was found dead in her dishwasher machine in Berkeley, California. It was no Maytag murder, the police determined, but a well-planned suicide. Carolyn had locked herself in her home, removed the internal racks from her washer, and stacked them neatly along with some personal effects. Then she set the machine to "on" and climbed in. The dishwasher started automatically when the lid was closed.

Quiz. *There are seven ways a baseball player can legally reach first base without getting a hit. Taking a base on balls—a walk—is one way. What are the other six? (Answer: page 121)*

HIS WIG WAS REAL

The three most enduring images of George Washington are the story of chopping down the cherry tree, the "Father, I cannot tell a lie" line, and the tale of him throwing (or skipping) a silver dollar across the Potomac. All three are entirely fictional.

The stories were made up by Mason Locke Weems, an itinerant preacher and bookseller, for a biography of Washington that he wrote in 1800. The book was enormously popular, and historian Daniel Boorstin has called it "perhaps the most widely read, most influential book ever written about American history." Weems, who certainly could tell a lie, single-handedly created the most popular legends about our first President.

Lunar material brought to earth by astronauts Armstrong, Aldrin, and Collins has been named Black Armalcolite in their honor.

Mozart's burial place is unknown.

In all boxing history, what is the shortest fight on record? One might think that 11 seconds should be the shortest possible time—one second for the punch and ten for the count—but in fact the shortest fight in history was even briefer than that. On September 2, 1957, Teddy Barker of England hit Bob Roberts of Nigeria just after the opening bell of a welterweight bout in Maesteg, Wales. Roberts collapsed, but was back on his feet before the count began. The referee decided that Roberts didn't look as if he could defend himself, so he stopped the fight and awarded the victory to Barker on a technical knockout. Elapsed time? Less than seven seconds.

When Dick Clark's first wife saw a new pop singer named Ernest Evans, she remarked that his appearance was like another famous performer. "He's like a little Fats Domino—a 'Chubby Checker,'" she said. Evans liked the idea and immediately adopted the new name.

PIANO-PLAYING MARATHON RECORD

Heinz Arntz began playing a piano in a Düsseldorf cafe on August 18, 1967, and didn't stop until the following October 1 at the Long Island Industrial Fair in Roosevelt, New York. The sixty-seven-year-old pianist rested only two hours each day during the forty-four day marathon, which included passage across the Atlantic on the steamship United States. "From now on, I think I'll play concerts," Arntz said after his finale.

Chester Carlson, who invented the xerography copying process in 1937, also had an idea for another important tool—but gave up work on it after concluding it wouldn't work. The idea later became the ballpoint pen.

Many may believe that a dictionary with Webster's in its title is connected with the famous dictionary created by Noah Webster. A book title can't be copyrighted, however, so any publisher can issue a dictionary with Webster's in the title, and many do.

Avant-garde musician John Cage composed a piece titled Imaginary Landscape No. 4. It is scored for twelve radios tuned at random.

The Tower of London was a prison whose famous inmates included Sir Walter Raleigh, Mary, Queen of Scots, and Lady Jane Grey. The last prisoner to be locked up there was Nazi leader Rudolf Hess. He was captured after parachuting into England during World War II.

The English word "testimony" comes from the Roman custom of a man putting his right hand on his testicles when swearing to tell the truth.

BORDER TOWNS

Texhoma is a little town in Oklahoma's panhandle that, as you might have guessed, is on the Texas-Oklahoma border. Calexico is a town in California just across the border from its more famous neighbor to the south, Mexicali.

The best-known border city of this type, Texarkana, Texas, is misnamed. When the community was founded in the 1870s, it was thought to be located at the juncture of three states, so a unique triple coinage blended them all: Texas, Arkansas, and Louisiana. The town is on the border of the first two states, but it turned out that the Louisiana line was about a hundred and fifty miles away.

The Palace of the Governors in Santa Fe, New Mexico, was built in 1610, ten years before the Mayflower landed in Massachusetts. Santa Fe is the oldest seat of government in the United States, even though New Mexico wasn't admitted to the Union until 1912. ~Photo by Mark Nohl, courtesy of New Mexico Economic and Tourism Department

Quiz Answers

Page 110: Kitty Litter.

Page 111: In Minnesota. The franchise, originally known as the Minneapolis Lakers, kept the name when it moved West. Similarly, the New Orleans Jazz kept its name when it moved to Utah. The jazz in Salt Lake City is about as notable as the lakes in Los Angeles.

Page 114: It's a corn butterer. Just put a square of Grade A into the chamber and press down on the top to squeeze a controlled amount of butter onto a hot ear of corn.

Page 116: Human blood temperature, which defined the hundred point. Fahrenheit was somewhat off in his measurements: the temperature of human blood was later set more accurately at 98.6 degrees on his scale.

Page 118: (1) Batter hit by pitch, (2) passed ball, (3) catcher interference, (4) catcher drops third strike, (5) fielder's choice, and (6)—the one that most fans don't get—being designated as a pinch runner.

A three-month-old pelican weighs more than a full-grown pelican. A fledgling bird consumes about a hundred and fifty pounds of fish in its first three months of life—the young birds need the extra fat to survive while they learn to fish for themselves. When young pelicans do leave the nest, they outweigh their parents. ~Photo by Leon Boltin, courtesy of Department of Library Services, American Museum of Natural History

CHAPTER
9

Mating octopuses don't touch each other with their genitals. Instead, the male octopus ejaculates onto one of his own tentacles and then places the sperm manually into the female's sex organ.

He called Bill Smith a liar.
~tombstone epitaph in Cripple Creek, Colorado

Jean Harlow died while trying to induce her own abortion. The child had been fathered by actor William Powell.

One historical legend that is true, after all, is the story about Isaac Newton and the apple. Newton himself told of seeing an apple fall one moonlit evening, which set him to wondering if the apple and the moon were held in the same force. Thus began his deliberations on the laws of gravity. The apple didn't hit Newton on the head, though: storytellers added that embellishment later.

A shrimp has more than a hundred pairs of chromosomes in each cell nucleus. A human being has only twenty-three.

OUTSCORED

Franz Joseph Haydn once challenged Wolfgang Amadeus Mozart to write a piano piece that Haydn couldn't play at first sight. The bet was for a bottle of champagne. Mozart dashed off a deceptively simple composition which Haydn confidently sat down to play. At the midpoint of the piece, Haydn found himself with his arms stretched wide on the keyboard while a middle note was supposed to be played simultaneously. He gave up in disgust. "Nobody can play such music!" he said.

Mozart sat at the piano and began to play his score. When he got to the passage calling for outstretched arms, he struck the middle note with his nose.

That night at dinner, Haydn bought the champagne.

When her conscience began bothering her, a San Francisco woman went to her priest to confess that she had embezzled $30,000 from her employer. The trouble was that her employer was the very church in which she was confessing. The priest turned her in to the authorities and she was eventually sentenced to seven months behind bars.

The woman later tried to sue the priest for $5 million for violation of confidentiality. "I needed to talk to someone, and the only person I could speak with was my priest," the woman said. She claimed that she had every right to expect forgiveness and absolution for her sins, even from a priest who was a victim of those sins. She didn't collect.

There's a crater on the moon called O.S., named by the astronauts of Apollo 15. Located across a twelve-hundred-foot-deep gully beyond their intended landing site, it got its name after the exclamation the astronauts would have had to make if their spacecraft landed there—"Oh, shit! We missed!"

Bolivia has had over 190 governments in 160 years.

What do a cat, a camel, and a giraffe have in common? Their walk. They are the only four-legged animals that move legs on opposite sides of the body at the same time: when the right foreleg moves forward, so does the left hind leg, and vice versa. Other quadrupeds walk both right legs at once, then both left legs, and so on.

A shower of tiny green frogs once fell in Greece. Scientists at the Meteorological Institute in Athens believe the frogs were sucked from a marsh in North Africa by a whirlwind and blown five hundred miles across the Mediterranean to Greece, where they fell to earth. Most of the frogs were uninjured, quickly adapted to the new environment, and settled in.

a certain type serves as a float. Several others combine to form the tentacles for fishing. A third variety digests the fish that the tentacles catch, and a fourth type is responsible for reproduction.

Quiz· *It's the only vegetable or fruit that is never sold frozen, canned, processed, cooked, or in any other form but fresh. What is it? (Answer: page 137)*

SLAVES OF PUNCTUATION

From 1850, Michigan's constitution read, "Neither slavery nor involuntary servitude, unless for the punishment of a crime, shall ever be tolerated in this state." For over a century this passage stood, apparently legalizing slavery as an appropriate punishment for a crime. It wasn't until 1963 that the punctuation error was noticed and the comma after "servitude" was moved to a position after "slavery," where it made slavery illegal.

The jellyfish known as the Portuguese man-of-war is not a single animal. It's actually a colony of several animals, all of the same species, but each adapted to perform specific labors. One animal of

THE ZAMBIAN SPACE PROGRAM

The space race wasn't just between the United States and the Soviet Union. The African nation of Zambia wanted to be counted in, early on, and Minister of Space Nkoloso once announced that there would be a Zambian man on the moon by 1970. Reporters were invited to observe the training of Zambian astronauts, which included rolling downhill in an oil drum and being whirled in a barrel tethered to a tree. These exercises were to teach the future astronauts what to expect in orbital flight. The men also learned to walk on their hands because, the minister said, that was "the only way humans can walk on the moon."

SOUPY FOR THE DEFENSE

Leon L. Louie, a Navy Seabee, was court-martialed for smashing a chocolate cream pie into the face of Chief Warrant Officer Timothy P. Curtin. Louie and his bored buddies at the Port Hueneme, California, base argued that the stunt was devised "to boost morale," but the Navy didn't buy it. Louie was the first person in the history of the U.S. Navy to be court-martialed for pie-throwing.

The trial was held in December 1974, and Louie's attorney called in Soupy Sales as a star witness for the defense. The kidvid comedian testified that he had personally received over nineteen thousand pies in the face since 1950. "It's the thing you can really do to relieve tension without hurting anybody," he said.

When news got to England that U.S. President George Washington had died overseas, British ships in the English Channel honored their former adversary by firing a twenty-gun salute.

NANOOK OF THE NORTH

One of the earliest documentary films, released over sixty-five years ago, was Nanook, the story of an Eskimo hunter and his family as they struggle to survive in the Arctic. The film is a remarkable record of a harsh way of life. Two years after this movie classic was made, the "star" himself, the Eskimo Nanook, died of starvation. ~Courtesy of Culver Pictures

The silver that went into the minting of the first U.S. coins came from Martha Washington's table settings.

BLACKOUT BABY BOOM A BUST

A massive power failure that hit New York in November 1965 was followed, the story goes, by a huge increase in the birthrate nine months later. Presumably, on the Night the Lights Went Out, couples went to bed early, and with no television to distract them they did what comes naturally. About nine months later, the New York Times reported an increase in births at Mt. Sinai Hospital on August 8, 1966.

The story is part of modern mythology, but it isn't true, according to J. Richard Udry, director of the Carolina Population Center at the University of North Carolina. The Times item may have been accurate, but it was just one day at one hospital—a random variation. Udry collected data from several New York area hospitals, tallied births between July 27 and August 14 of 1966, and compared them to births between the same dates from 1960 to 1965. His conclusion, reported in the journal Demography (August 1970), was that the birth-

rate nine months after the blackout was slightly below the five-year average.

Nonetheless, the story of the Blackout Baby Boom has been repeated so often that it is still widely believed, even in the face of evidence that it never happened.

From our "Nothing New Under the Sun" file come these two observations about the trouble with youth:

> Children are now tyrants. . . . They no longer rise when elders enter the room. They contradict their parents, chatter before company . . . and tyrannize over their teachers.

> What is happening to our young people? They disrespect their elders, they disobey their parents. They ignore the law. They riot in the streets inflamed with wild notions. Their morals are decaying. What is to become of them?

The words sound like modern laments about "the problem with kids today," but the sentiments are ancient. The first dire warning is from Socrates, the second is from Plato, talking about the moral decline of his own students.

OLD WIVES' TALES

There is no evidence whatsoever that cedar chests or closets act as moth repellents.

127

Years after his famous ride, the legendary American patriot Paul Revere ended his military career in disgrace. He was the commander of a garrison of soldiers who participated in the Penobscot Expedition, a naval raid against British forces in Maine in 1779. The attempted invasion was a fiasco, many ships were lost, and Revere was blamed. The legendary hero was court-martialed for cowardice and insubordination. Though he was cleared of all charges he quit the military under a cloud and never quite lived down the scandal.

Quiz· *Seymour the snake is ten feet long plus half his own length. How long is Seymour? (Answer: page 137)*

In 1946 the Republicans from one Southern California congressional district placed the following ad in several area newspapers: "WANTED: Congressman candidate with no previous political experience to defeat a man who has represented the District in the House for 10 years. Any young man, resident of district, preferably a veteran, fair education, may apply for the job."

One man saw the ad in the Whittier, California, paper, and thought it sounded like a good opportunity. He answered the ad, got the Republican nomination, and defeated congressman Jerry Voorhis in a dirty campaign with accusations of Voorhis' Communist leanings. The man who started his political career by answering a newspaper ad: Richard M. Nixon.

WHATEVER HE DID, HE DID IT WELL

Leslie C. Dirks received a mysterious National Security Medal from President Carter in 1979. Dirks, the CIA's deputy director for science and technology, was cited for "his outstanding contribution in creating and directing a major intelligence program of great national importance." Reporters and photographers were barred from the ceremony, and the White House press office said it had no idea why Dirks received the medal because the information was classified.

❝ Nolan Ryan is pitching much better now that he has his curveball straightened out. ❞
~Joe Garagiola

Asked his opinion of jogging, ex-astronaut Neil Armstrong said, "I believe every human has a finite number of heartbeats. I don't intend to waste any of mine running around doing exercises."

Quiz. *Which of these seven regions of the continental United States has the greatest percentage of forested land—Pacific Coast, Rocky Mountain, Central, Great Lakes and Dakotas, Southern, Mid-Atlantic, or New England? (Answer: page 137)*

Modern astro-folklore claims that the Great Wall of China is the only man-made feature on Earth that is visible from the moon. This is "common knowledge," but it's utterly false. Arthur N. Waldron of Princeton University's East Asian Studies Department debunked the myth in a 1983 letter to the *New York Times*. No astronauts have ever said they could see the Great Wall even from Earth orbit, much less from the moon. "And in any case," Waldron wrote, "a few calculations demonstrate the idea's absurdity. According to my friend Dr. Alta Walker of the U.S. Geographical Survey, seeing the Wall from the moon is like seeing a Popsicle stick from 384 kilometers [238 miles]."

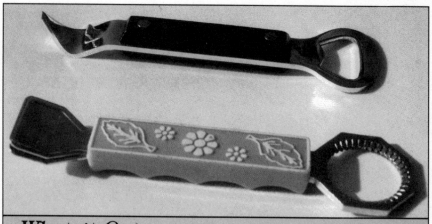

Whatzit Quiz

The tool at the top is an old-fashioned "church key," the left end used for opening cans, the right end for prying off bottle tops. What is the tool at the bottom? (Answer: page 137) ~Photo by Scot Morris

On June 16, 1948, a Cathay Pacific Airways flying boat, en route from Macao to Hong Kong, was seized by a gang of Chinese bandits led by one Wong-Yu Man. The gang planned to hold the passengers for ransom, but the pilot fought them off and in the ensuing struggle the airplane crashed. The only survivor was Wong-Yu Man. That was the tragic outcome of the world's first recorded airplane hijacking.

Ancel Keys was a professor of physiological hygiene at the Mayo Foundation at the University of Minnesota. He is respected for having created a nutritionally correct food that soldiers could eat in the field. It was barely edible, but one could survive on it. Millions of U.S. soldiers learned to hate the taste of the concoction named after the doctor who invented it: K ration.

After you reach adulthood, your spinal cord discs lose their elasticity and become compressed. Year by year you shrink. Old people can be as much as three inches shorter than they were in their prime.

PATENT NOT PENDING OR APPLIED FOR

Chemist John Walker never patented his invention of matches because he believed the idea should belong to the world. For the same reason, Pierre and Marie Curie never took out a patent on their process for isolating radium. They thought the results of their work should be owned by all mankind.

Christopher Columbus' first transatlantic voyage was accomplished at a speed of about 2.8 m.p.h.

A SKEPTIC SPEAKS

“ Is there anyone anywhere so foolish as to think there are Antipodeans—men who stand with their feet opposite to ours, men with their legs in the air and their heads hanging down? Can there be a place on earth where things are upside down, where the trees grow downwards, and the rain, hail, and snow fall upward? The mad idea that the earth is round is the cause of . . . this imbecile legend. **”**

~Lactantius Firmianus, tutor to the son of Emperor Constantine the Great of Rome, 304 A.D.

The song "Rosanna," by rock group Toto, was written to actress Rosanna Arquette.

The largest island in the world is Greenland, which lies within the Arctic Circle and is usually white with ice and snow. Any greening there occurs in coastal areas only during the brief summer season. Viking explorers deliberately gave the island a misleading name to trick settlers into moving there.

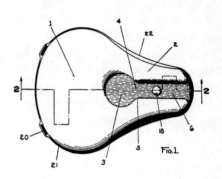

Fig. 1.

Thomas Edison averaged one new patent every two weeks of his adult life.

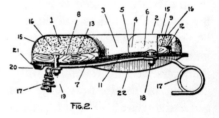

Fig. 2.

Apollo 8 astronauts used a new adhesive to fasten down their tools during weightlessness—Silly Putty.

Quiz. What animal has the highest blood pressure? You might guess this one right if you give it some thought. (Answer: page 137)

A BICYCLE SEAT FOR THE SENSITIVE MAN

Fred Blake of Indianapolis found that after riding a bicycle he was sore in the most personal part of his body. He invented this improved bicycle and motorcycle seat "having a suitable cavity properly located to allow comfortable clearance for the private organs of the male rider." He got U.S. Patent No. 1,538,542 for his idea in 1925. ~Reproduced with permission from *Mousetraps and Muffling Cups* by Kenneth Lasson

Speaking English was once outlawed in Illinois. A bill passed by the state legislature in 1935 declared, "The official language of the State of Illinois shall be known hereafter as the American language" (*Illinois Revised Statutes* [1935], Chapter 127, Paragraph 177).

HERE'S TO YOUR HEALTH

In many European hospitals, the first food given to patients after abdominal surgery is champagne. The doctors find that this is the only form of nourishment that the stomach can take and hold after the trauma of an operation.

TURNPIKE TACTICS

In order to see if those lane-changing speed demons one often sees on the freeway really reach their destinations faster than the rest of us, the Los Angeles police set up a test of driving technique on the Hollywood Freeway. Four cars were to travel ten miles in traffic on the freeway. One was allowed to dart back and forth between lanes at will, the others could go as fast as possible without changing lanes. The result? The speed demon finished only eighty-two seconds ahead of the slowest of the other three finishers.

In 1878, when Thomas Edison was thirty-one, his reputation as an inventor was already so great that when he announced that he would try to invent an electric light bulb, the price of lighting gas stock crashed in New York and London.

CASE OF THE KILLER PIANO

The Condor nightclub in San Francisco is famous for the topless dances of silicone-implanted Carol Doda, often on the club's hydraulically operated elevator piano, which raises her high above the stage.

Recently the piano was involved in a bizarre accident. James Ferrozzo, assistant manager of the Condor, was having after-hours sex with his girlfriend atop the piano when their gyrations activated the elevator mechanism and they started to rise. They were apparently too distracted or too drunk to worry until it was too late. Ferrozzo died of asphyxiation by being pressed between his girlfriend and the ceiling, but the girl survived with only bruises. A janitor found them fifteen feet above the floor the next morning. It took the fire department nearly three hours to rescue the girl. She said she had had so many drinks she couldn't remember any of what had happened.

Variety reported the story with the headline EXEC OF TOPLESS CLUB DIES IN FREAK ACCIDENT WITH PIANO, WOMAN. The story concluded on another page, under the line HE DIED HAPPY.

A SHADOWY TRADITION

.{On February 2, known as Candlemas Day, Christians celebrate the purification of the Virgin Mary after giving birth to the Baby Jesus. A medieval tradition, with obscure origins and no basis in meteorological fact, held that the weather on that day would be a kind of reverse predictor of the weather to come. A cold, cloudy day indicated there would be an early spring, but sunny skies meant there would be several more weeks of winter weather. The legend held that on this day hibernating animals went outside to check the weather. If a hedgehog could see his shadow on Candlemas Day, farmers delayed planting their fields for a few weeks.

The custom of observing February 2 is carried on in America, but with an entirely different animal. Since the spiny hedgehogs aren't found on this continent, the North American groundhog, or woodchuck, has been assigned to fill in for the sake of tradition. No matter that the two animals aren't closely related at all, the groundhog has proved to have the same weather-prognosticating ability as the English hedgehog—that is to say, none at all.

My work is done. Why wait?
~suicide note left by George Eastman (1854–1932), the founder of Kodak

The largest cell in the human body is a female's egg cell, the ovum. The smallest human cell is a male sperm.

ONE LAST DETAIL BEFORE TURNING OUT THE LIGHTS

Representative Cletha Deatherage once introduced a bill in the Oklahoma House of Representatives that would require a man to obtain a woman's written consent before they engaged in sexual intercourse and to inform her that she could become pregnant, which could result in serious health problems.

·{ What's the difference between neurotic and *psychotic*? Many distinctions have been drawn, but we like this, by Dr. Karl Menninger: "Neurotic means he's not as sensible as I am. Psychotic means he's even worse than my brother-in-law."

other insisted on total abstinence. Members were identified on the roll as "O.P." (for Old Pledge) if they promised to drink moderately and "T—Total" if they swore off entirely. The latter group soon became known as teetotalers.

WHERE RONNIE STOOD

❝I favor the Civil Rights Act of 1964 and it must be enforced at gunpoint if necessary.**❞**
~Ronald Reagan, 1965

❝I would have voted against the Civil Rights Act of 1964.**❞**
~Ronald Reagan, 1968

{ Cut a starfish into several chunks and each piece will grow back into a complete starfish.

·{ Marie Antoinette was bothered by the fact that handkerchiefs came in all sizes and shapes—some triangular, some round, some rectangular, and so on. After due and careful deliberation, she decided that handkerchiefs should be square, so she prevailed on her husband, Louis XVI, to issue a law to that effect. On June 2, 1785, the King decreed that henceforth "the length of handkerchiefs shall equal their width, throughout my entire kingdom." All because of the King of France, it is virtually impossible to buy a nonsquare handkerchief today.

In the 1830s, a Michigan temperance society offered its members two pledges—one allowed moderate drinking and the

NAMETOPPERS

{ The five most common surnames in North America are, in order: Smith, Johnson, Williams, Brown, and Jones.

Quiz· Under a strong light, stare at the spot in the center of the drawing above. Hold the book steady, and be careful not to move your head or your eyes while you stare at the spot. After twenty or thirty seconds, look at a blank piece of paper or a white wall. You'll see something quite unexpected. What is it? (Answer: page 137)

135

The Alabama State Court of Appeals once ruled it a crime to call anyone either a skunk or Adolf Hitler.

In 1911, three men were hanged in London for the murder of Sir Edmund Berry at Greenberry Hill. The murderers' names were Green, Berry, and Hill.

SACRILEGIOUS CEREAL

In 1904, when C. W. Post marketed a new cereal called "Elijah's Manna" he was criticized by churchmen for naming his product after God's gift to Israel. So Post gave his breakfast food a less controversial name: "Post Toasties."

When producer Irving Thalberg's first son was born, Eddie Cantor sent the moviemaker this telegram:
CONGRATULATIONS ON YOUR LATEST PRODUCTION. AM SURE IT WILL LOOK BETTER AFTER IT'S BEEN CUT.

"JUST A DROP?"

Never make the mistake of thinking that a drop is an approximate measurement. There are 60 drops in a teaspoon, 120 in a dessert spoon, 240 in a tablespoon, 480 in an ounce, 960 in a wineglass, 1,920 in a teacup, 3,840 in a tumbler, 7,680 in a pint, 15,360 in a quart, 61,440 in a gallon, 2,935,360 in a barrel, and 3,870,720 in a hogshead. An official drop of water weighs .9493 gram.

It was agreed by the Union and the Confederacy that George Washington's beautiful plantation at Mount Vernon would be considered neutral territory. No armies invaded it during the Civil War.

BULLPEN BULL'S-EYE

In the 1965 All-Star baseball game, Pittsburgh Pirate Hall of Famer Willie Stargell hit a powerful home run. The ball landed inside a tuba in the right field bullpen, where the members of a marching band were practicing.

Quiz Answers

Page 125: Lettuce, the most popular green vegetable in the world.

Page 128: Twenty feet long.

Page 129: New England is easily the most forested region, where trees cover up to 81 percent of the available area. Forests fill 58 percent of the Mid-Atlantic states, but less than 40 percent in the next most woody areas, the South and the Pacific Coast. Trees are sparsest in the Central region, where they cover only 18 percent of the area.

Page 129: The bottom tool does exactly the same things on "new" cans and bottles. Beer and soda cans now have tab-tops, which ironically were supposed to do away with the need for the pointed end of a church key. The slotted end of this new tool is for gripping tab-tops and prying them up without breaking your fingernails.

Bottles now have twist-off tops, which were originally introduced to do away with the need for the other end of the church key. The circular end of the new tool is to help open stubborn twist-off tops without skinning your hands. Is this progress?

Page 131: The giraffe, whose blood pressure is two or three times greater than a human's. Because of the force needed to pump blood up ten to twelve feet of neck, the giraffe's heart is enormous: it weighs twenty-five pounds and has walls up to three inches thick.

Page 135: This amazing design is used by psychologists to demonstrate the phenomenon of after-image. After staring at a fixed image for several seconds, your eyes become fatigued: shift your gaze to a neutral background and the parts of your retina that saw black will now see white, and vice versa. The "negative" image is immediately recognized as Leonardo da Vinci's famous portrait of the Mona Lisa.

CHAPTER

10

One of the strangest movies ever filmed was The Life of General Villa, a documentary on Mexican guerrilla leader Pancho Villa, who conducted a real revolution, in 1914, under the direction of Hollywood moviemakers. Villa got $25,000 in gold in return for the right to film him during the uprising he was leading against the Mexican dictator General Victoriano Huerta in Mexico City.

The battle scenes were directed by Raoul Walsh, who became famous as the director of such Hollywood classics as What Price Glory? and High Sierra. Villa would hold up his battles until Walsh got his cameras into position. Walsh got Villa to delay all battles until 9 A.M., when the sunlight was right, and to stop fighting after 4 P.M., when the light grew too dim to film. Sometimes the director got Villa to stop a battle in the middle, until the cameras could be moved to a new angle, and then to resume the killing when the filmmaker was ready for "Action!"

No prints of the movie survive.
~Photo courtesy of Culver Pictures

A MINOR TECHNICALITY

Thomas Jefferson believed that his Louisiana Purchase agreement with Napoleon was unconstitutional. Even so, he urged congressmen to ratify it anyway and to put "metaphysical subtleties" behind them.

Rabies is a virus infection that attacks the nervous system. An afflicted animal cannot swallow, and the attempt to do so throws it into a convulsion. The ancient Greeks misunderstood the disease and thought that the convulsions came from a fear of water. That's why they gave rabies such a misleading name—"hydrophobia."

Karate is a combat technique usually identified with Japan. Ironically, it was first developed centuries ago by Okinawans to defend themselves against the Japanese. Karate was not introduced to Japan until 1916.

The rudimentary intermaxillary bone in man was discovered in 1784. The jawbone became important to Darwin's theory of evolution a century later. The discoverer was a scientist who was better known as a writer—he was Johann Wolfgang von Goethe, Germany's most celebrated literary figure and the author of *Faust*.

THE QUEST FOR A SEE-THROUGH FROG

"It's not easy being green," said Kermit the Frog, and animal lover Ernest Ebbitson of Hertfordshire, England, agrees. He has spent over thirty years breeding a species of orange frogs. The light color makes their skin almost transparent. "You can see right through them," Ebbitson says. "It's like looking at an X ray."

Why does he want a see-through frog? "To end the wanton dissection of frogs at universities where thousands are used each year," he says.

FLASH! SICK PEOPLE USE DOCTORS MORE THAN HEALTHY PEOPLE DO!

It cost $180,000 for the U.S. Health Resources Administration to come up with a report on health care that led to the conclusion that "individuals in poor health were almost seven times as frequent users of physician services as those in excellent health, and spent an average of 21 times as many days in the hospital."

This study almost makes the Department of Agriculture look thrifty. It funded a survey that concluded mothers prefer children's clothing that doesn't have to be ironed; the bill was $113,417.

Divide your weight by six to get the approximate number of quarts of blood in your body.

The weasel and the ermine are not just close relatives, they're the same animal. An ermine is just a weasel whose coat has turned white for the winter. The white version of the animal's fur is much preferred: there's just not much call for weasel coats.

140

.{ "Pennsylvania 6-5000" was a hit song for Glenn Miller. The title was the telephone number of the Hotel Pennsylvania (now the Penta) in New York City, where Miller's orchestra often played.

Quiz· *How is it possible for a pitcher to make four or more strikeouts in one inning?* (Answer: page 152)

Camels aren't native to America, of course, but for a while in the 1850s herds of wild camels could be seen roaming the American West. It all started as the pet project of Jefferson Davis, long before he became the leader of the Confederacy, when he was Secretary of War in President Franklin Pierce's cabinet. Davis wanted to test the animals' usefulness in the American desert, so he arranged a joint army-navy project that brought thirty-four camels to America and landed them in Texas. The military expeditions Davis planned didn't pan out and the project was scrapped. Some camels were set loose, to roam the American desert on their own; others ended up being used in farming jobs or even for racing. (A camel can beat a quarter horse in a race over a short distance.) ~Photo by F. Puza, courtesy of Department Library Sciences, American Museum of Natural History

In April 1954, U.S. tumbler Dick Browning reportedly did a back somersault over a high bar set at seven feet six inches. At that time, the world high-jump record was six feet eleven and a half inches. In 1962, when the Olympic high-jump record was seven feet one inch, Gary Chamberlain did a back handspring with a back flip over a bar set at seven feet four inches and landed on his feet. These achievements never made it into the track and field record books, however, because one of the official rules for high-jump events is that competitors must take off from one foot only, and these gymnasts sprang from two.

HOW TO CARAMEL-COAT A CEILING

In 1978 Random House published a new cookbook, *Woman's Day Crockery Cuisine*, that contained a dangerous recipe for caramel slices. It was discovered that because of the omission of a single ingredient in the recipe—water—anyone who followed the book's directions to the letter could cause a can of condensed milk to explode. Random House had to recall ten thousand copies of the cookbook to correct the potentially lethal recipe.

What's the name of the famous clock in the tower at the Houses of Parliament in London? It's not Big Ben but the Tower Clock. Big Ben is the name of the thirteen-ton bell, the largest forged at its time, which rings the hours in the clock. ~Photo courtesy of British Tourist Authority

SMASHING STONES

{ Emeralds are unbreakable, or so believed Francisco Pizarro's Spanish army in Peru in 1532. When soldiers found large green stones they smashed them to bits with hammers and concluded the finds were only colored glass. Their belief was mistaken and in "testing" the jewels they destroyed countless genuine emeralds, some reportedly as large as pigeon's eggs.

{ When James Dean speaks in the drunken banquet scene in Giant, the voice on the soundtrack isn't his. The producers found that Dean's mumbled lines were inaudible in the original scene, but he had already suffered his fatal auto accident when they decided to redub it. Actor Nick Adams got a hundred dollars a day for three days' dubbing, impersonating the voice of the dead screen idol.

{ A 13,905-foot-high mountain in Canada's Yukon Territory is named Mount Kennedy, after the late U.S. President. It was climbed for the first time in 1965. A member of that first expedition to the summit was Robert Kennedy.

{ Charles Darwin predicted the discovery of an exotic insect he never saw. When he visited Madagascar on the voyage of the Beagle, he studied a shiny white orchid so large that he theorized it could only be pollinated by an unknown insect with a foot-long proboscis.

Darwin was ridiculed for his preposterous theory until twenty years later, when a nocturnal moth with a five-and-a-half-inch wingspan and a twelve-inch proboscis was collected for the first time on Madagascar. Darwin's prediction was commemorated in the name given to the insect—Xanthopan morganii praedicta.

{ John Paul Jones was a legendary American naval hero, but he was not quite the hero type. Born out of wedlock in Scotland, and named just John Paul, he joined an acting troupe in Jamaica, worked as a pirate, committed two murders, and then lived under an assumed name (he added the "Jones" to escape detection). He was tried for rape in Russia and died penniless in France, where he was buried. His remains were exhumed a century later, through the efforts of ambassador Horace Porter, and today are enshrined at Annapolis.

INFIELD ERROR

Baseball is a game of inches, they say, and perhaps the strangest inches in the game are in the official distance between the pitcher's mound and home plate—sixty feet, six inches. Why the six inches?

It all dates back to 1893, when the decision was made to change the official pitching distance on professional baseball fields from fifty to sixty feet. A hand-drawn diagram used to plot the dimensions noted the distance as 60' 0", but the surveyor who laid out the field read the "0" as a "6" and set the distance at 60' 6". When the mistake was discovered, it was too late. The odd measurement became "official," and the extra six inches stayed in every professional baseball field built ever since.

Hunters in Connecticut killed 948 deer during 1978. In that same year over a thousand deer in the state were killed accidentally by automobile drivers.

A chameleon takes on the color of its background even if it can't see. A totally blind chameleon placed on a blue cloth still turns blue.

*R*udolph the Red-Nosed Reindeer, whose glowing nose was pressed into service by St. Nick one foggy Christmas Eve, is becoming as much a part of the Christmas legend as Santa Claus himself. Rudolph was created fairly recently, by a department store advertising man with a flair for light verse.

In 1939, when Montgomery Ward was looking for something their in-store Santas could give to children, they went to advertising copywriter Robert May and asked him to compose a Christmas poem. He came up with the legend of Rudolph. Santa's ninth reindeer became an institution ten years later when Gene Autry recorded Johnny Marks' musical version of the poem and the record reached the top of the hit parade.

Sociologist James Barnett sees Rudolph as a variation of the ugly duckling motif, and a symbol to children of the comforting lesson "Whoever you are, you're special." The Rudolf legend, he says, is "the only original addition to the folklore of Santa Claus in this century." ~Photo courtesy of Culver Pictures

❝ I can see stopping a car for a dog. But a cat? You squish a cat and go on. I think we're overcomplicating life. **❞**

~State Senator James Gallagher, in 1980, on a proposed Iowa law that would require drivers who hit a domestic animal to stop and give aid

Cary Grant's real name, before he entered show business and changed it, was Archie Leach. In *His Girl Friday* (1940) Grant poked fun at himself with the line, "The last person to say that to me was Archie Leach, just before he cut his throat."

GERM WARFARE USED AGAINST INDIANS

After Chief Pontiac destroyed a number of British forts in the American colonies in 1763, the British retaliated in a devastating way. They deliberately infected Pontiac's Ottawa tribe with smallpox by giving them contaminated blankets and handkerchiefs they obtained from a hospital.

The weight of the sun's light on the earth's surface has been determined to be two pounds per square mile.

REAPING SALES BENEFITS

Cyrus McCormick invented the reaper, as every schoolchild knows, but he also came up with an economic innovation that was even more lasting. To make it easier for farmers to buy his invention McCormick originated the idea of buying on the installment plan.

Quiz. Many countries have changed their names —Persia is now Iran, Ceylon became Sri Lanka, and Northern Rhodesia changed to Zambia, for example. But only one country we know of has officially changed its pronunciation. What is it? (Answer: page 152)

❝ My dear fellow, I may perhaps be dead from the neck up, but rack my brains as I may I can't see why a chap should need 30 pages to describe how he turns over in bed before going to sleep. **❞**

~editor Marc Humblot to Marcel Proust, rejecting *À la Recherche du Temps Perdu* (*Remembrance of Things Past*) for publication, February 10, 1912

TESTIMONIAL

·{ When he was Vice President, Walter Mondale wrote a letter of recommendation for the Reverend Jim Jones, leader of the People's Temple. Jones presented the letter to the government of Guyana, which allowed him to set up his ill-fated, suicidal religious commune there. Mondale's letter positively glowed with admiration. "Knowing of your congregation's deep involvement in the major social and constitutional issues of our country is a great inspiration to me," the Vice President wrote.

§ Less than 5 percent of the paperwork filed in the average office is ever seen again by anyone for any reason.

❝ If you eat bananas, your skin will exude an odor which is very attractive to mosquitoes. ❞
   ~warning from the Canadian national park service

Geraldine Farrar, of New York's Metropolitan Opera Company, once starred in a most peculiar movie. Filmed in 1915, it was a silent film version of the opera Carmen.

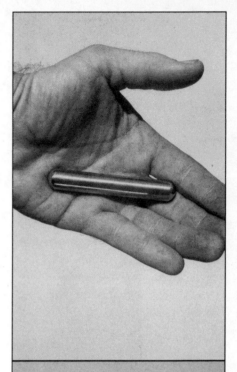

Whatzit Quiz

In the previous "Whatzits" you saw a picture of a tool and had to come up with its name—usually two words that fully described its use (spaghetti measurer, cork sharpener, corn butterer, etc.). On this final Whatzit we give you both the picture and the name.

The shiny cylinder shown is a high-quality Alnico magnet, about two and a half inches long, and rounded at the ends. It is called a cow magnet.

How is a cow magnet used? (Answer: page 152) ~Photo by Scot Morris

Meredith Willson is best known for writing *The Music Man*, but he had other musical credits as well. He was first flutist with the New York Philharmonic, under Arturo Toscanini. He also wrote the music for Charlie Chaplin's *The Great Dictator* and for Lillian Hellman's *The Little Foxes*.

Quiz. Name ten parts of the body that are spelled with only three letters. (No slang or dirty words!) (Answer: page 152)

"Even the most uncompromising champion of the rights and capacities of women must admit that in contests of physical skill, speed, and endurance they must remain forever the weaker sex," editorialized the *London Daily News* on August 6, 1926.

Gertrude Ederle couldn't read the editorial, however, because on that very date she was in the water, swimming the English Channel in a record time of fourteen hours and thirty-one minutes. The American teenager's time was almost two hours faster than the previous record—held by a man named Enrique Tiraboschi.

Thousands of hamsters have been used in research experiments in the United States and England. Virtually all of them are descended from a single litter captured in Syria in 1930.

DWINDLING DIET

A century ago mankind lived on forty to fifty different crops around the world. Today we have narrowed our diets so that only a dozen plants provide the bulk of all human nutrition: corn, wheat, barley, soybeans, potatoes, rice, millet, sorghum, oats, rye, peas, and peanuts.

It's the fat in beef and pork that gives them their characteristic tastes. If all the fat were removed from these meats, the Department of Agriculture says, you wouldn't be able to taste any difference between them.

When I was a young man, I vowed never to marry until I found the ideal woman. Well, I found her. But, alas, she was waiting for the ideal man.
~Robert Schumann

If Alexander Graham Bell had been a late sleeper, people might have cursed "Ma Gray" when they opened their telephone bills years later. Elisha Gray submitted to the U.S. Patent Office a description of his invention, the telephone, just a few hours after Bell delivered his own. Maybe if Gray had left a wake-up call . . .

When oil was discovered in the United States in 1859 it was a valuable source for such products as kerosene, naphtha, and petroleum jelly. One by-product, gasoline, was at first discarded as a nuisance. There was no practical use for it until years later, when the automobile was invented.

CHOCOLATE CONNECTION

A candy bar in a scientist's pocket led to the invention of the microwave oven. When Percy LeBaron Spencer of Raytheon realized that microwave signals had melted the candy in his pocket, Raytheon looked into the phenomenon and marketed the first microwave oven in 1947.

Mothballs in your tool chest will keep tools from rusting.

"HE'S DEAD, JIM"

It's a movie cliché. The doctor's face drops as he lifts the eyelids of an accident victim. "We're too late," he says sadly. In fact, there is absolutely no way to tell whether a victim is dead or just unconscious merely by looking at his eyes.

From 1836 to 1896, the Red Flag Act in England required any self-propelled vehicle to be preceded by a man carrying a red flag by day and a red lantern by night. This limited speed to four miles per hour. This single law, according to Isaac Asimov, set the development of the automobile back for decades.

The name Key West doesn't come from this key being the farthest west, which it is, but from an English corruption of the original name, Cayo Hueso. The Spaniards named it after the piles of unburied human bones they found there. Cayo means "islet," hueso means "bone." It was the Island of Bones.

Quiz· Can you name six or more articles worn on the feet that start with the letter s? (Answer: page 152)

❝A city of Southern efficiency and Northern charm.**❞**
~John F. Kennedy, describing Washington, D.C.

HITLER'S ARROGANT "VICTORY JIG" A HOAX

Have you seen films of Adolf Hitler doing a silly little dance when France surrendered at Compiègne in June 1940? Millions saw it in movie theater newsreels that summer, and millions more have seen it in reruns of World War II news films.

It never happened. In German films of the Führer, Hitler is seen to jump in astonishment once, in response to hearing about the surrender. Allied propagandists "looped" that instant of Nazi film, running it back and forth, over and over, for the version released to newsreels. It created the illusion that Hitler acted childishly, dancing a silly "victory jig" over the defeated French. It was all a hoax, perpetrated by Allied film editors, to fool the millions of Americans who saw movie newsreels every week.   ~Photo courtesy of American Heritage Picture Collection

THREADS IN NECKTIES DECODED

·{G}old and silver threads are often woven into the lining of neckties. The threads vary in number from one to six, and indicate the weight of the fabric in the tie's lining. One thread denotes the lightest fabric, six the heaviest.

Quiz. Where can you find the Island of Reil, the Islets of Langerhans, the Crescent of Gianuzzi, the Canal of Gugier, the Pyramids of Malpighi, and the Crypts of Lieberkühn? (Answer: page 152)

The Cathedral of St. Basil the Beatified in Moscow is one of the world's most impressive buildings. It is said that in 1555 Ivan the Terrible had the architects blinded so they could never design anything more beautiful. (When the author, at right, was in Moscow in 1988, he asked a tour guide about this story and was told, "It's a legend, widely believed in the West, but not true.") ~Photo by Dottie O'Carroll

"WHAT ONE MAN CAN IMAGINE, ANOTHER CAN DO."

~Jules Verne

There are amazing similarities between Jules Verne's fictional *From the Earth to the Moon*, written in 1865, and the Apollo 11 moon flight in 1969.

Verne's rocket blasted off from Cape Town, Florida, which isn't far from the Cape Canaveral launchpad used over a century later.

Verne's spacecraft held a crew of three and was named *Columbiad*. There were also three astronauts in the Apollo command module, the *Columbia*.

The expeditions reached the moon within five hours of each other: Verne's took four days and one hour and Apollo made the trip in four days and six hours.

Verne's spacemen ate meat and vegetables "reduced by strong hydraulic pressure to the smallest possible dimensions," and the real astronauts also ate capsules of concentrated food.

paint a landscape showing twelve hundred miles along the Mississippi River.

He camped along the Mississippi and made thousands of sketches for a year, then returned to his studio in Louisville. Banvard installed a rolled-up mile of canvas that he would unroll, paint, and then roll again as a finished painting onto a huge spool.

When his colossal work was finished in 1846, it was exhibited in Louisville to great acclaim and then toured the United States and Great Britain. Banvard's artistic feat became world-renowned and made him wealthy, but the painting disappeared after his death. Parts of it were last seen as stage scenery in Watertown, South Dakota. No photographs of the painting are known to exist.

A "spermologer" doesn't study sperm. The word means a collector of trivial or unusual data.

THE BIG PICTURE

An American artist named John Banvard (1815–91) created a picture on an unbroken mile-long canvas. It was Banvard's idea to

Morology is the study of foolishness. The author of this book is a part-time morologist and spermologer. If you have read this far you probably are, too.

Quiz Answers

Page 141: If the catcher drops a called third strike and doesn't throw the batter out at first base, the runner is safe.

Page 145: Kenya. It was formerly "KEEN-ya," but now the name is pronounced "KEN-ya," to rhyme with the last name of leader Jomo Kenyatta.

Page 146: Farmers will feed a cow magnet to a young calf, and for a good reason. Grazing cattle often swallow sharp pieces of metal—nails, bits of baling wire, barbed wire, etc. If these pass through a cow's body, they can cause serious injuries—a syndrome that veterinarians call "hardware disease." The cow magnet stays in a cow's first stomach (there are four), where it collects all the bits of metal the cow swallows, preventing them from passing on into the digestive system. One magnet can protect a cow from hardware disease for its entire lifetime. When the animal is slaughtered, the farmer can reclaim the magnet for use on another calf. The accumulated scrap metal in a mature cow can reach the size of a baseball.

Page 147: The ten simplest are arm, ear, eye, gum, hip, jaw, leg, lip, rib, and toe. Other possibilities include gut, lid, and fat.

Page 149: Shoes, socks, sandals, sneakers, slippers, skis, snowshoes, stockings, and so on.

Page 150: They are all parts of the human body, listed in Gray's Anatomy and named after the anatomists who identified them.

INDEX